Words on the Air

John Sparrow

WORDS ON THE AIR

COLLINS
St James's Place, London
1981

William Collins Sons & Co Ltd
London · Glasgow · Sydney · Auckland
Toronto · Johannesburg

British Library CIP data
Sparrow, John
  Words on the air.
  1. English literature
  I. Title
  824'.9'14   PR6037.P31

First published 1981
© John Sparrow 1981
ISBN 0 00 216876 6

Phototypeset in Linotron 202 Palatino by
Western Printing Services Ltd, Bristol
Made and Printed in Great Britain by
William Collins Sons & Co Ltd Glasgow

Contents

Contents

Foreword

The pieces collected in this book qualify as *Words on the Air* because all (but one) of them are printed records (with virtually no alteration) of the spoken word. *The Sin of Pride* is a sermon preached in the University Church at Oxford on 23 November 1975; *Good English* was delivered as the Presidential Address at the Annual General Meeting of the English Association on 21 June 1980 and published by the Association, with whose permission it is here reprinted; the concluding three pieces, *Too Much of a Good Thing*, were delivered as the Sara Halle Schaffner Lectures at the University of Chicago in 1976 and published in 1977 by the Chicago University Press; they are here reprinted with the permission of the University. All the other pieces were broadcast during the years 1977–1980 on the Third Programme of the BBC, except *Marcuse and the Gospel of Hate*, which appeared in *The Spectator*, 9 August 1969.

Words

Short Words

I thought I might call this first talk of mine on Words 'The Long and the Short of it', or 'A few short words on Words', and I hope that quite soon, as I go on, all of you—or most of you—will see why it was that I thought of those names.

Let me say, to start with, that I love words. I have loved them since I was a boy. So, of course, I was glad to have a chance to hold forth on them on the air. But, I must say, it made me think. I can't just say 'I love words', and leave it at that. What do I mean when I say I love words? And why do I love them? I don't mean—at least I hope I don't mean—just that I love the sound of my own voice. I do love that sound, no doubt, and I hope (by the way) that you like it too, or (at least) that you don't find that it grates on your ears. But there is more to it than that. I have to ask: what is it in words that I love? And what, when one comes to think of it, does the word 'word' mean? What *is* a word? It's not just a sound. Is it a sound that stands for a thing? But not all words stand for things—lots of them don't. Take the words 'and', 'the', 'not',—none of these words stands for a thing. Words, I should say, are best thought of as *parts of speech*. (I won't say more on this now, but I may next time.) Well! These were the kinds of doubt that rose up in my mind when I sat down to write this talk. Then I thought 'First things first!' Let's take it stage by stage, and keep the hard things—'What do words *mean*?', 'What *is* a word?', 'What, if it comes to that, is a *thing*?', and so on—let's keep all that till the end.

They say—don't they?—that one should not use long words: short words are best—best for *sound*, best for *sense*, best for *use*. And there's a good deal in this. Up to a point, it is quite true. One *can* go on for a long time—I dare say one could do it for half an hour or more, if one put one's mind to it—and use no long words at all.

I don't know if it has got through to you—no, I won't put it like that; that sounds rude, as though it were your fault: 'Have I got it through to your thick heads?', that kind of thing, and that's not what I mean at all. What I mean is that I don't know if it's dawned on you, but it is the fact that all the words I have used so far in this talk have been as short as short can be. As I've just said, I think I could go on like this for half an hour, or I dare say for a whole hour. But there comes a point, and I have reached that point, when one longs to burst out, as I now burst out, with a polysyllable—dramatically, significantly, appropriately.

I admit that it's a great relief to be allowed to use words of two or more syllables. To be confined to using monosyllables imposes on one a considerable restraint—it limits the range of possible effects. But one can be moving even in monosyllables. Take the following—which surely wouldn't disgrace the most eloquent of pulpit orators:

> Christ died on the Cross. Though He was God, the Lord Most High, He deigned to come down from the skies to dwell on earth with us men, to live with us, to work with us, to serve us, and—in the end—to save us, so that when we come to die our souls shall not be lost in Hell, as the price of our sins.
>
> That was God's way with man.
>
> And how did we men treat Our Lord when He came to live with us on earth? What did we do to Him? We scourged Him; we spat on Him; we crowned Him with thorns—and we killed Him.
>
> That was man's way with God.

I think you'll agree that that's hard to beat.

Here is something rather different—a racy dialogue which surely loses nothing in liveliness by being entirely composed of words of one syllable:

'Hold your tongue or else get out of here, you

young fool!' 'Why do you call me young? Do you know how old I am?' 'No, I don't; and I don't care what your age may be. I *do* know that you are a fool'. 'Well, if I'm a *young* fool, you are an *old* one—and that's a far worse thing to be. There's no fool like an old fool—and if *you* weren't an old fool, you'd know it'.

Well! my five minutes is up, and I suppose I must terminate my peroration, finish my discourse, come to an end, or just, monosyllabically, stop.

Vogue Words

There is a fashion in words, as there is in everything else. It isn't only that styles of speech change, that formal diction comes to seem stilted and is replaced by modern slang; there is also a fashion in individual words. Particular words, often pretentious, high-sounding, words, get taken up and come into general use—they become 'vogue' words. Why do some words come in and others go out? It is difficult to say. Let me give one or two examples of words that seem to me to be in vogue to-day.

Why do people nowadays say 'simplistic', when they mean 'simple', or perhaps 'simplified'? Why do they talk about a 'paradigm case' when they mean a 'typical example'? Why do they use the word 'parameter' when they mean (or I suppose they mean) 'shape' or 'outline'? Why do they talk about something 'escalating', and what do they mean by it? I read an account the other day of a meeting at which a controversial subject was introduced; 'and that' (said the reporter) 'escalated the confrontation'. He meant, I suppose, that the discussion got heated and out of hand. Why couldn't he have said so? Why do people talk this strange language? I suppose some people use pretentious words—'paradigm', 'parameter', 'simplistic', and so on—in order to impress other people, and then these words get taken up by other people who want to seem in the swim. They become vogue words. The process, with the help of the 'media'—broadcasting, TV, and the popular press—is an increasingly rapid one: words come into vogue very quickly nowadays.

One of the most fashionable of 'vogue' words today is the word 'dialogue'. In the old days, when two people got together to discuss something, one said that they discussed it, or talked it over: people now call any exchange of views a 'dialogue'. It sounds grander, and it has a classical ring: perhaps they think that since a speech by one person is called a 'monologue', a 'dialogue' means a discussion between two people—which only shows that they do not know Greek.

Often, a 'dialogue' is said to be a 'dialogue in depth'. What does 'in depth' mean? Usually, nothing at all. It is just a fashionable phrase. I saw the other day a report by a student on his work—his field was English Literature—in which he said 'I have glanced in some depth at Greek Tragedy'. 'Glanced in depth'! How deep, one wonders, can his glance have gone?

Then, there is the word 'dynamic', used not as an adjective but as a noun. Not long ago, I met a parent who said that he had never punished his children. Why not? 'Well', he said, 'it sets up a wrong dynamic in the nursery'. Again, I read a publisher's 'blurb' the other day, which declared: 'The message of this book is relevant anywhere because it pin-points the generation gap'. Relevant to what? The writer meant 'important'—but 'relevant' is a vogue word. And 'pin-point': that's a popular word because it suggests scientific precision—but how precisely can you pin-point a gap?

Another vogue word is 'viable'. People are always calling things 'viable': 'That idea isn't viable'; 'It is not a viable scheme'. What do they mean? They mean, I think, that the thing isn't practicable, that it won't work. Why can't they say so? 'Viable' has a classical ring: I suppose they think it comes from the Latin word *via*, which, as a matter of fact, it does not.

Finally—and I have kept the worst to the last— what about 'syndrome'? Here is a word which no doubt has a technical meaning for the physiologist and the psychologist. Its history is rather like that of the word 'complex'. When psychoanalysis first came into fashion, the word 'complex' was taken up and used by people who didn't really know what it meant: 'He must have a complex about it', they would say, meaning that someone was obsessed with something. It was one of the vogue words that came to stay, and it stayed long after its psychological origin had been forgotten. In the phrase 'inferiority complex' it has its accepted place in our vocabulary.

So with 'syndrome': it is commonly used nowadays by people who haven't the faintest idea of its true meaning—and who don't really know what they mean by it when they use it themselves. 'He gets up later every morning.' 'Oh! that's a very common syndrome.' 'The familiar oil and vinegar syndrome.'

A day or two ago I saw a publisher's announcement of a forthcoming book. It was called *Syndromes of the Seventies*. I wonder what it contained!

Of course, the word 'syndrome' has a classical

ring that no doubt makes it impressive; but its classical associations may lead people sadly astray. Everyone knows that a Hippodrome is a place of public entertainment, like the Coliseum. May not Palindrome, like the Palladium, be another name for the same thing? And didn't Coleridge begin *Kubla Khan* with the words:

> 'In Xanadu did Kubla Khan
> A stately pleasuredrome decree'?

Blurred recollection of all these 'dromes' may explain the exchange I overheard the other day on the top of a bus. 'I can't think where they can have met,' said one lady. 'Oh', replied her friend, 'I believe he picked her up at that big new Syndrome just off the King's Road.'

A 'Sindrome'—a pleasure-palace, where nothing is forbidden—will that word some day take its place in the language by the side of 'inferiority complex'? Hadn't we better banish it right away, and stick to plain English?

Jargon

The other day I received two letters—both of them, I may say, from the other side of the Atlantic—containing testimonials in support of a candidate for an academic post. One of them, from a Professor of Political Science, said that the candidate was *'capable of forming insightful associations between the elements of his knowledge'*; the other, from a Professor of Economics, said that he was *'sophisticated in interpersonal relationships'*. What they meant, I suppose, was that the candidate was shrewd,—he could put two and two together—and that he was sensitive about people. Why couldn't they have said so?

Why can't people use simple, familiar words when they want to convey simple, familiar ideas? Why must they use stilted phrases (like *'the elements of his knowledge'*) and invent monstrous words (like *'insightful'* and *'interpersonal'*)? Oddly enough, academics and educationists—people, you might think, who ought to know better—seem to be particularly prone to this abuse of language: they are always using words like 'interdisciplinary' and 'cross-fertilization'. A month or two ago I read an address on Art and Education delivered at an international Congress by an English County Advisor for Art and Design. He talked a lot of twaddle about Art ('I believe that Art represents a unique aspect of human consciousness that should be experienced if we believe in the human condition', and so forth), and then, getting down to brass tacks about the actual business of teaching, he said this: 'The teacher does have a very significant and positive rôle. Indeed it would be dangerously near to educational abdication to equate a pupil-centred approach with unstructured learning situations.'

I suppose this means that if you think that taking an interest in the personalities of your pupils involves letting them dictate the syllabus, you might as well give up trying to educate them. But what a way of putting it! '*A significant and positive role*', a '*pupil-centred approach*', which is to be '*equated*' with '*unstructured learning situations*'!—if teachers write like this, how will their pupils write?

Here's another example of educationists' English, from a document put out by a County Association of Headmasters of Secondary Schools. They define a disruptive pupil as '*one who makes it impossible for an orderly teaching situation to obtain*', and who '*is not contained by the discipline structure appertaining to the particular school*'. '*Situation*' again!—this time a '*teaching situation*' instead

18

of a *'learning situation'*—and a *'discipline structure'* instead of an *'unstructured situation'*.

Why do they write like this? I don't think they do it in order to impress their readers; it's their natural mode of speech; it's a sort of jargon. The danger is, that they may get taken in by it themselves; it saves them the trouble of precise thought.

Of course, most professions have a jargon of their own, a sort of short-hand or code-language that makes verbal communication between their members easier and quicker. That's all right, so long as they don't become victims of their own vocabulary, but are able to translate it into plain English for the benefit of non-experts.

Not long ago I received a circular from the Department of Industry, inviting my College to send them *'details of any Terotechnology related items which may be included in your programme'*. *'Terotechnology related items'*? What a phrase! And *'Terotechnology'*: what on earth did it mean? Well, they supplied a definition: Terotechnology is *'a combination of management, financial, engineering and other practices applied to physical assets in pursuit of economic life-cycle costs'*. What can one say to that? *Obscurum per obscurius*. I suppose the Terotechnologists could have translated it into other, simple, intelligible terms.

Sometimes people use jargon in order to soften

19

or to mask a harsh or an unpleasant reality. I was recently invited to attend a symposium organized by the Eugenics Society. What was it to be about? Well! the title told me nothing: it was called 'Perimeters of Social Repair'. 'Perimeters'! I suppose we should be grateful to them for not having said 'Parameters', which would have been equally meaningless—at least, to me. And what is 'Social Repair'? The title of the opening lecture—Dr Pamela Poppleton on 'Models of Social Repair: Myths and Dilemmas'—didn't help; indeed, it made me suspect that the whole thing was a hoax. But one could gather from the rest of the programme that it was concerned with the care and education of backward, half-witted, children; wicked, 'delinquent', children; children from broken homes; human misfits—what are nowadays called, euphemistically, 'disadvantaged' children. That was what the symposium was about, and it couldn't have had a worthier or a more important subject. Why then this pretentious, circumlocutory title?

The organisers of 'Perimeters of Social Repair' just couldn't bring themselves to call a spade a spade. But often I find the pronouncements of idealistic academics and educationists literally meaningless. Take this, from a prospectus that reached me not long ago from a body that calls itself CEVAM—the 'Center for the Exploration of

Values and Meaning'—and has its headquarters in Indianapolis. '*CEVAM* (I am quoting) *is an Institution which continually researches, contemplates, and evaluates its own restructuring*'.

What are its aims?

They are (I quote again) to discover:

'*What are the structures that will enhance society;*

How institutions reinforce certain values and limit other values; and

What is the nature of leadership that it will reinforce values?'

In case you are in doubt about the principles that govern CEVAM's activities, the prospectus re-assures you: its basic principle is this:

Core human values are transcultural but are expressed in cultural modes.

Finally, the goal of the Institution's activities is

To originate new methodologies for a more effective realization of value choices.

How, you may ask, can intelligent, educated, self-respecting human beings—the staff of CEVAM consists largely of Professors and Deans and Directors of University Departments, with a strong infusion of clerics (there is a Bishop among them)—how can people like that lend their names to such a disgusting programme, and devote their time and their energies to working for it? If there were money in it, one could understand; but

CEVAM is a non-profit making institution, and those who work for it are not, I am sure, thinking about what they can make out of it. No: I am afraid that what is proved by the programme of CEVAM is that language was given us not only as a means of expressing our thought, and of concealing or disguising our thought, but also in order to provide us, on occasion, with a substitute for the thinking process.

CEVAM, you may say, is so far away in the clouds that it can't do any harm to anyone. But when 'educationists' put out nonsense of this kind, one trembles for their pupils. I was looking the other day at the programme of a course organized by a New York Educational Foundation based (it was said) on 'recent research conducted in major educational institutions into useable ideas'. The course offered 'Encouragement through participation in an exemplary climate for optimum stimulation of creative effort'. Its aim was to provide, among other things, 'an orientation in creative evaluation', proceeding by 'morphological or matrix approaches to idea-finding' (with the aid of 'the Osborn checklist of idea-spurring questions'), to such 'specializations' as Value Engineering and Sensitivity Training. What can go on in schools run by people who talk like that?

At the morning session of the fourth day of the

22

course, according to the programme, *'Evaluation criteria will be explored. Synthesis and creative evaluation will be practiced. Refreshments will be served'*— a reassuring touch of reality to end up with!

'With It' Words

Far too many people, as we all know, are given to using unnecessarily long, pompous-sounding words. Sometimes they do it deliberately, in order to impress the person they are talking to; more often they do it because they've got into the habit, it has become a second nature to them; they are the victims of their own inflated vocabulary.

But there's an opposite vice, not so generally recognized, which is just as common, and which I myself find just as irritating: people go out of their way to use plain, short words and colloquial phrases, because they want to give an impression of directness, familiarity, heartiness, cosiness— an impression of being 'with it'.

The other day I was looking at a pamphlet published by the B.M.A. called *Happy Marriages*. In it

23

the authors, one of whom was an Anglican Bishop, was offering advice to people about to get married. One of the things that the happy couple were advised to attend to in relation to the impending ceremony was this: *Make sure that both Mums have settled their outfits*. What it meant, of course, was 'Make sure that both the prospective mothers-in-law have decided what they are going to wear at the wedding'. But—'Mums'? 'Outfits'? Surely those words didn't come naturally to the lips of the Bishop, or his colleagues? I am afraid they were simply talking down to their audience.

Sometimes people use this sort of language just in order to create a familiar, homely atmosphere; of course they're not condescending; they are only trying to reassure their audience: 'We are all friends together!' I am told that BBC announcers, if there is a minute or two to spare at the end of the News, will hand over to a meteorological colleague with the words: '*John Smith will now fill us in with the weather*'. Well! there's nothing particularly wrong with this, but I must say that it strikes me as a disagreeable affectation, a sort of inverted linguistic snobbery.

There is another use of colloquialism which seems to me to be getting very common nowadays. Of course people have always been prone, when they don't quite know what they mean, to use a long word to conceal the woolliness of their thought. Nowadays, I have noticed, they are inclined to use a colloquialism to jolly you along, so to speak, past a gap in their sequence of ideas.

A word that is very often made use of for this purpose is the word 'about'. That short and simple preposition is made to cover a multitude, not of sins, but of undigested ideas: a speaker—and it is often in public speaking that this aberration occurs—is not 'talking down', he is *covering up*. He wants to plead for some cause, or to justify some course of action, that he thinks important, and he wants to do it by reference to a high aim or ideal that commends itself to everyone: his trouble is that he can't find a rational link between the two. What does he do? He falls back on 'about'. That poor little word must be breaking under the strain that has been imposed upon it during the past few years. Politicians and advertisers are the worst offenders. Let me give you one or two examples. One of the last two or three leaders of the Liberal Party crowned an eloquent plea for what he called 'Participation' with the words 'Participation is surely what democracy is supposed to be about'. Another statesman, I won't say of what party, after giving an enthusiastic review of the benefits to be expected from our joining the Common Market, wound up with the words 'That's what Europe is about!' You can use 'about' like this in almost any context, to

25

commend any sort of merchandise or any sort of cause: to persuade people to go to church, for instance—*'That's what Christianity is about!'*—or to support Independent Secondary Education—*'That's what the Public Schools are about!'*—I have seen both these in print.

The more elevated the subject, the more degrading is this horrid linguistic confidence trick. The nastiest example I have come across, I think, was in a charitable appeal with the worthiest imaginable object: *'Cancer relief'*, said the appeal, *'is about living'*. Surely the author of that sentence ought to be ashamed of himself?

I will end with a less serious example. It occurs in an advertisement sponsored by a leading firm of brewers, which is to be seen today on posters all over England. It represents a young man on a stool at the bar of a public-house, with a brimming tankard in his right hand and his left arm round the waist of a girl who is sitting on his lap. The caption is: *That's what Beer is about!*

Certainly, the advertisement is *about* beer; and the young man is *about* to drain his tankard; and his arm is *about* the girl's waist: and the girl is, probably, *about* to be kissed by the young man. But beer—whether the beer in his tankard or beer in general—beer isn't *about* anything.

Well! I dare say you feel you have heard enough

about this particular topic, and it is *about* time I drew to a close.

Monstrous Births

I want to talk to-day about monstrous births, or perhaps I should say mixed marriages, in the world of language—I mean, unnatural etymological compounds, and the hybrid words that they produce.

Some years ago I happened to be in a little town in Lancashire called Parr—PA double-R—and I found myself in front of the municipal theatre. What do you think it was called? It was called *The Parrvilion*. I must say, it gave me a nasty turn. Of course, I know, it was a sort of joke—a play upon words; one mustn't take it seriously; but it seemed to me a joke in bad taste, an etymological indecency.

Now, if I'd bought a ticket and gone into The Parrvilion, I should probably have been confronted by a young woman offering to sell me a programme and show me to my seat. And what would she have called herself? An *usherette*. Well!

I confess, the word 'usherette' makes me shudder. It reminds me of another monstrous birth—an American cousin of 'usherette'—that I once saw under a photograph showing a squad of frilly-skirted, high-stepping, young women on the march with drums slung from their shoulders which they were pounding in unison with drumsticks. What were they called? *Drum-majorettes*. Of course it's a sort of joke: one mustn't be pompous about it. But, I confess, I found the word and the picture equally distasteful.

When one is confronted by these hybrid words, it's often difficult to know how much of what one feels is distaste for the make-up of the word, and how much is distaste for what it stands for. No one minds 'cigarette'—a French diminutive of a French word standing for a perfectly acceptable object. What about 'Suffragette', a female supporter of the Votes for Women movement? I expect that sixty years ago I should have disapproved of the word and of what it stood for; but it was accepted into the language, became perfectly respectable—and has now become practically obsolete.

What about *'maisonette'*? You can't fault it etymologically any more than you can 'cigarette'—it is French from beginning to end. But it isn't a word, surely, that two English people would use in talking to each other—any more than they would use the phrase 'desirable residence'—unless one of them happened to be a house agent?

I think that what one objects to about these foreign intruders is not the fact that they are foreign, but the fact that they are used in order to give a (bogus) sense of something *chic*, something a bit better than the ordinary—a bit better than anything with a merely English name. So, a little laundry where you can do your own things is ashamed of being called a laundry and calls itself a 'launderette'—or even (God save the mark!) a 'washeteria'. Why do I shudder at these words? Not only because I think them odious etymological anomalies, but because I don't like the thought of some people using them to impress others, and other people being impressed by them.

But they do worm their way into the language, and corrupt it. People set up a shop, and attract custom by calling it, not just a 'shop', but a 'boutique'. What do you think I saw in Oxford the other day? A sign advertising a *Scootique*—a shop where you can buy scooters. Well! I know, it's half a joke. But the young people who buy a scooter at a scootique may well go on to the neighbouring *boutique* and ask—in all innocence—for a pair of boots.

Not far from the *Scootique* I came upon a shop where you could buy jeans. What do you think that was called? It was called a 'Jeanorama'; the

proprietors of the Jeanorama described themselves as 'the active jean people'.

Well! I suppose if I set up as an ironmonger,
who sells pots and pans, or a tinker, who mends
pans, I might call my place of business a 'Panor-
ama', and describe myself as 'an active pan person'. That may sound far-fetched and fantastic,
but remember the Parrvilion!

Another way in which manufacturers try to
impress their customers is by inventing, for the
things they make or sell, high-sounding technical
names with a pseudo-scientific ring—many of
them monstrous hybrids, impossible combina-
tions of Greek and Latin elements: let me mention
two that recently caught my eye: *instamatic* and
reprography.

If you don't know the difference between Greek
and Latin, you won't shudder, you won't feel
there's anything wrong with these monstrous
compounds—indeed, you may even be impressed
by them. Well! I am not proud of being able to
recognize the parentage of such hybrids and
being upset by them when I hear them used; but
ought I to be ashamed of it? There's supposed to
be something shameful nowadays about *discrimination*: one mustn't recognize differences, and
if one does recognize them, one must pretend that
they don't exist—there are actually laws against it
in the field of race and in the field of sex. Let us at
30

least preserve our right to discriminate in the field of language, and preserve the purity of our national speech.

Good English

"Good English': an appropriate subject, I should think everyone would agree, for the Address to be delivered at an Annual General Meeting of the English Association—and a temptingly easy subject, anyone might suppose, for the person who has the duty, and the privilege, of delivering that Address. So, indeed, I myself supposed, until I sat down and applied my mind to the task of composing it.

What do we mean by 'good English'? What did I mean by the phrase when I chose it as the title of to-day's discourse?

Well! to tell the truth, I hadn't realized, when I proposed that promising title, the difficulties, the problems, the ambiguities, that lie hid in those two simple words.

'Good English': of course, there's what one might call the pedagogue's use of the term—we recollect it, surely, many of us, from our school-days. How often the form-master in a preparatory school would interrupt a pupil with a sharp 'That's not good English!' What he meant, of course, was that the offender had broken one of the rules of grammar, or syntax, or vocabulary. 'Good English', in such a context, means 'correct English'—and if you talk about 'correct English' that means that you accept a set of rules as governing the use of the language.

From what source those rules derive their authority; how much they change, and in what respects they change, from age to age, even from decade to decade; and in what circumstances or contexts, while we acknowledge their validity as rules, it is permissible for us to break them— these, I think, are interesting and intriguing questions. The rules of grammar may surely, on occasion, be honoured in their breach rather than in their observance, indeed, the conscious breach of a rule, as distinct from an ignorant failure to obey it, may be a sort of tribute to its authority: for instance, I would suggest that it is possible to deliberately, effectively, even (dare I say it?) *felicitously*, split an infinitive.

That is the realm of language that the late Sir Ernest Gowers ruled as his demesne, having inherited it—one might say—from the brothers Fowler, whose pioneering (and classic) work on *Modern English Usage* first came out in 1926.

Gowers was a distinguished Civil Servant, and he was invited by the Treasury in the 1940s to help them in their endeavour to extirpate 'officialese', which had become the prevailing language of civil servants, Local Government officials, and the staffs of public bodies. The Treasury could not have chosen a better man. Gowers' *Plain Words* came out in 1948, and was followed by *The ABC of Plain Words* three years later. These were published together in 1954 as *The Complete Plain Words*, a compendium that has been reprinted, I don't know how many times, as a Penguin Book.

When Sir Ernest died in 1966 he had just completed revising the Fowlers' *Modern English Usage*. He was succeeded as sovereign ruler of the realm of the English language by Sir Bruce Fraser, who in 1973 brought out a revised and enlarged edition of *The Complete Plain Words*, which is now the sacred text for those who want to write good English.

The Fowlers, Sir Ernest Gowers, and Sir Bruce Fraser have succeeded in their main endeavour: they have exposed and discredited, if they haven't eliminated, 'officialese' in this country. Meanwhile, the good work has been carried on on the other side of the Atlantic. The pioneer in America was a Professor of English at Cornell, William Strunk, who used, in instructing his pupils, a 'little book'—*parvum opus*—which he had privately printed after the end of the first World War, called *The Elements of Style*.

Twice revised by a pupil of Strunk's, E. B.

White, in 1957 and again—simultaneously with Sir Bruce Fraser's *Complete Plain Words*—in 1973, it is still a little book, but in its small compass it teaches the same lessons as Sir Ernest Gowers and Sir Bruce Fraser: the virtues of straightforward, intelligible English—plain English, like, I am tempted to add (but would it be true? and would it be grammatical?), like I'm talking now.

Let me now explain, or do my best to explain, what I mean when I speak of the special pleasure I derive from reading (or hearing) good English. It has nothing to do with sound of the words. Are some words, are some languages, more beautiful, *to the ear*, than others? Italian than German? French than English? Yes! but the pleasure one gets from hearing a language spoken has very little to do with the *sound* of its words. 'Peace!'—said a venerable friend to me, when I was a child—'Peace!', and he repeated it, once, twice, thrice. 'The most beautiful word in the language! *Peace* of mind! The *peace* of God, which passeth understanding'. And I was duly impressed. But, on reflection, I couldn't help asking myself whether it was the word that was beautiful, or what it stood for. And I had to conclude that my venerable friend was deceiving himself. What about 'May I give you a *piece* of cod?'? Or, 'I'm going to give you a *piece* of my mind!'? The sound is the same—but hasn't the effect it produces on

35

the listener lost, in these contexts, something of its power to arouse emotion?

I couldn't begin to experience the special pleasure that I get from hearing a passage of what I call 'good English' if I didn't understand what was being said. On the other hand, that *special* pleasure isn't derived from the content, the thoughts or sentiments conveyed by the writer (or speaker); or, rather, it is not derived from the content alone: what makes me think of it as 'good English', and enjoy it as such, is the efficiency with which the words give expression to the meaning. A sentence that answered to Pope's definition of 'wit'— 'What oft was thought, but ne'er so well expressed'—would assuredly deserve to be praised as good English. But what about this—which you may recognize as the closing paragraph of *Wuthering Heights*?—

> I lingered round them, under the benign sky: watched the moths fluttering among the heath and hare-bells; listened to the soft wind breathing through the grass; and wondered how anyone could ever imagine unquiet slumbers for the sleepers in that quiet earth.

Perfect; beautiful; deeply moving—but, 'good English'? No one would think of so describing it. And that goes for all poetry, or for all poetry that deserves the name, and is not mere verse.

Let me give you another example:

> It is an owl that has been trained by the Graces. It is a bat that loves the morning light. It is the aerial reflection of a dolphin. It is the tender domestication of a trout.

That surely is an amusing and beautiful piece of English. It is suffused with humour and its humour depends, of course, upon its meaning, upon the sequence of the ideas of pictures— absurd, paradoxical, pleasing—that Ruskin presents us with. Why do I call it beautiful? Not because of the sound of the words: someone who didn't understand the words wouldn't (I think) take any particular pleasure in hearing the sound of them. Nor in the meaning—it isn't beautiful (like, say, the concluding sentences of *Wuthering Heights*) because of the emotional message it conveys, the feelings that it arouses. Its beauty, I think, consists in the choice of words, the suitability of the words to the picture they present: the monosyllabic, myopic, owl—'Ten low words oft creep in one dull line'—here, ten low words lead up to the light concluding trochee, 'Graces'. The blind bat—seven monosyllables again, leading up to the climactic 'morning light'—('It is a bat that loves the dawn' would be hopeless). Then, 'the aerial reflection of a dolphin': the lightness of the syllables itself reflects the lightness it describes. Finally, the 'tender domestication of a trout': good English—yes! but something more than that!

At this point, I hope you will forgive me if I introduce an informal interlude. Only the other day I acquired a volume just published by the University of California Press, called *The State of the Language*, in which more than sixty writers, English and American, men and women, raise and explore all sorts of fascinating issues concerning 'English To-day', under a variety of headings—Proprieties, Identities, Media and the Arts, Societies etc. etc.

I was tempted to devote the rest of my Address to a discussion of the issues raised in one or two of these essays, particularly the first, in which the Quain Professor of English Language and Literature at University College, London, pleads for what he calls a 'discoursal' reflection of three contemporary 'norms', which he sums up as '(a) a concerned sympathy for others, particularly the perceived underdog; (b) a contempt for hypocrisy; and (c) an existential determination to explore human experience to the fearless limits of individual need.'

'Four letter words for all!' or, as he puts it, 'The porn merchants, like the poor, have always been with us . . . we must take the roughnecks with the smoothies and accept that any major social move-

ment will spawn its deviants. Taken as a whole'
(he concludes) 'I remain convinced that the sociolinguistic health of English speakers now is in
better shape than when Dickens could congratu-
late himself on avoiding speech that might 'offend
the ear'.' I was sorely tempted to take up the
Professor on these points: I felt concerned, I
confess, about his own 'sociolinguistic health'.

But that would have meant scrapping the
almost completed draft of my Address, and laun-
ching into a discussion that could have taken me
into deep and difficult waters , and I might have
been ship-wrecked.

Discretion is the better part of valour—and I
hope you will forgive me if I take a more cowardly
course and illustrate my conception of Good
English by putting before you half-a dozen actual
examples of what seems to me to be English at its
best—Good English, so to speak, at work, in action, fulfilling one or other of the various purposes—contention and argument, narration and
description and reflection— that language can be
made to serve.

For the last forty or fifty years I have kept a
commonplace book, copying into it things that
seemed to me specially pleasing, or moving, or
amusing, or impressive. I should like to submit to
your judgement, as specimens of good English,
a few extracts from that very miscellaneous

compilation. They are, of course, passages of prose, not poetry—and not poetic prose—not fine writing, not specially emotional or moving passages, but just good plain prose, prose that tells a story, or expounds an argument, or describes the writers' surroundings, or his state of mind, prose that conveys economically and effectively what it was that the writer or speaker wanted to communicate—and conveys it in such a way that the reader or listener feels—or, I think, ought to feel—and I hope you *will* feel—a thrill of pleasure as he recognizes how well the thing is done.

Before I turn to my commonplace book, however, let me start with a piece that everybody knows; the rest of my examples I hope may be unfamiliar to most of you, if not to you all. The first, the familiar one, is from Dr Johnson. Dr Johnson, as we all know, had two styles—and he knew it himself; 'He seemed', said Boswell, 'to take pleasure in speaking in his own style', and when he slipped carelessly into everyday speech he would often correct himself and translate what he had said into Johnsonian diction: as when he said of Buckingham's *Rehearsal* 'It has not wit enough to keep it sweet'—and then—recollecting himself and his vocabulary—'It has not vitality enough to preserve it from putrefaction'.

For the piece I am going to quote—an example of English used as a weapon of contention—

Johnson chose an every-day, forthright, un-Johnsonian diction: it is his famous letter to James Macpherson. Macpherson, you will remember, fraudulently claimed to have discovered and translated the text of Ossian, the primitive Gaelic epic poet. Johnson expressed his incredulity; Macpherson, he suggested, was perpetrating a fraud upon the public, and he challenged him to produce his originals. Macpherson wrote Johnson an angry, threatening, letter, to which Johnson replied as follows:

> Mr James Macpherson,
> I received your foolish and impudent letter. Any violence offered me I shall do my best to repel; and what I cannot do for myself, the law shall do for me. I hope I shall never be deterred from detecting what I think a cheat, by the menaces of a ruffian.
> What would you have me retract? I thought your book an imposture; I think it an imposture still. For this opinion I have given my reasons to the publick, which I here dare you to refute. Your rage I defy. Your abilities, since your Homer, are not so formidable; and what I hear of your morals, inclines me to pay regard not to what you shall say, but to what you shall prove. You may print this if you will.
>
> SAM. JOHNSON.

Well! there are 131 words in that letter, three of them four syllables long, seven of them three

41

syllables long; *the remaining hundred and twenty-one are all of them words of one or two syllables only*.

I won't attempt to analyze the text of the letter and account for its effectiveness—but I would just draw attention to the opening phrase: 'I received your foolish and impudent letter'. 'I received', you will observe; not 'I have received'. Somehow, that preterite puts Macpherson, as it were, at a distance; it depersonalizes the exchange of letters; not 'I have received your letter and I hasten to reply to it', but 'Your letter reached me—and here is my answer'—and it is, surely, an unanswerable answer?

The next passage that I want to read tells a story: it is good English at, I think, its *narrative* best. It is to be found in the *Literary Recollections* of Richard Warner, which were published in 1830. Warner is described in the *Dictionary of National Biography* as a 'divine and antiquary'; he was born in the 1760s and lived to be over 90. For more than twenty years round the turn of the century he was incumbent of a parish in Bath; he was the best known man of letters in that city, a learned antiquarian, a friend of Dr Parr, and the author of a large number of historical and topographical works, notably a series of 'Walks' through the Western counties, most of them published with charming aquatint illustrations. As a young man, in the 1790s, he served as a curate under William

Gilpin, Prebendary of Salisbury and Vicar of Boldre in Hampshire, and it is Gilpin who is the hero—or should I say the anti-hero?—of the little story that I now quote from Warner's *Recollections*.

> Among Gilpin's publications [says Warner] was a pamphlet entitled *An Account of William Baker*, which came out in 1790. It is mortifying to reflect [he continues] that with regard to the subject of this pamphlet, (who was a real character), the worthy and unsuspecting Vicar of Boldre should have been the dupe of vulgar artifice, and consummate hypocrisy, concealed under the cloak of apparent blunt candour and rugged honesty. William Baker was an old rustic, resident in a wild part of the parish of Boldre. In one of his walks, Mr Gilpin had lighted upon his cottage. On entering it, he found its inhabitant , an aged, but stout and athletic man, eating his humble dinner. All within was neat and clean: and something indicative of strong sense, and a cheerful mind, appeared in the countenance of the old peasant. Mr Gilpin sat down, informed Baker who he was, and entered into conversation with him. He soon perceived that his host, though without much education, was a man of clear head and strong mind: *abnormis sapiens, crassaque Minerva*; well versed in the Bible; full of maxims of prudence and economy; and apparently, of the most open, blunt, and independent character. Highly interested by his visit, Mr Gilpin frequently repeated it; and from the conversations which

passed, during this intercourse, between Baker and himself, he drew up that beautiful account which he published in the pamphlet above mentioned. The misapprehension of Baker's real character, was not done away, till some time after the death of the old man; and considering it as exemplary, at the time of his decease, Mr Gilpin wrote a short epitaph; and had it engraven on Baker's tombstone, as a salutary monition to the parishioners of Boldre. At length, however, he was undeceived; and had the sorrow, rather than the mortification, to find, that Baker had been, through life, a worthless and flagitious character: that age, instead of curing, had only altered the nature of his vices; and that by all, except the pastor, he had ever been known, and despised, as a consummate rogue, an oppressive extortioner, and a base hypocrite.

Surely that is an excellent example of English used to good narrative effect? I wouldn't want to alter a word of it.

Now let me read to you what I hope you will agree is a beautiful piece of *descriptive* prose. It was written by a Scottish judge, Lord Cockburn. But it is not a specimen of judicial English: it wasn't spoken from the Bench. Cockburn was born in 1779 and died in 1854. After his death his executors brought out several volumes of his Reminiscences, which give a fascinating account of the legal and the literary world of Edinburgh in the

first half of the last century—the world of Walter
Scott and Brougham and Jeffrey and Dugald
Stewart. Cockburn's *Memorials* is a book that de-
serves to be better known than it is, I think, to-day.
The passage I am going to quote comes from his
Circuit Journeys, in which he presents a series of
vivid pictures of life in and about the Scottish
law-courts; it is the closing passage of the book.

Cockburn had been trying a harrowing case in
which one Alexander Cunningham was charged
with the murder of his wife. He was convicted,
and sentenced to death by Cockburn (says
Cockburn's biographer) 'in a most impressive
manner'.

Our last criminal case (one of murder) was over
[says Cockburn] about two o'clock of the afternoon of Thursday, the 20th. I left Ivory [Lord
Ivory was his fellow-judge on the circuit] to try a
civil cause, and, passing by the back of the Court,
found myself on the sea shore. It was one of the
finest days even of this unsurpassed spring. The
beautiful bay of Ayr could scarcely have been
more beautiful. The advancing sea was insinu-
ating its clear waters irresistibly, yet gently, into
the innumerable little hollows and channels of
the dry sand. Few people were out, but plenty
sea-fowls playing on the beach, and in the air,
and with the long soft waves. Three white-
skinned boys were bathing. No ship, not even a
boat, was visible. There was no sound, except of

45

an occasional hammer by a few lazy masons who were pretending to be repairing the point of the pier, the ring of whose implements only deepened the silence. The picture of repose was completed on reaching the pier, every projecting point of which was occupied by one or two old bodies of rod fishers, who were watching the bobbing of their corks, as attentively as slumber would allow. They caught nothing, and said that they would not till it should rain, which it had not done for six weeks. So the very fishes were at rest too. It was all a refreshing contrast to the heat and crowd of that horrid Court.

That was written on the 22nd of April, 1854; next day, Cockburn was seized with a serious illness, and within four days he was dead.

My next example is also a piece of judicial English— in this case, strictly judicial English, for it was spoken from the Bench; but it is not concerned with legal technicalities; it sums up in plain language a story that the layman can understand as easily as the lawyer. It is an extract from the speech of Lord Macnaghten in the case of *Gluckstein v Barnes*, which came before the House of Lords in 1900. The relevant facts, and the point at issue in the case, appear very clearly from the following passage from Lord Macnaghten's speech:

These gentlemen set about forming a company to pay them a handsome sum for taking off their hands a property which they had contracted to buy with that end in view. They bring the company into existence by means of the usual machinery. They appoint themselves sole guardians and protectors of this creature of theirs, half-fledged and just struggling into life, bound hand and foot while yet unborn by contracts tending to their private advantage, and so fashioned by its makers that it could only act by their hands and only see through their eyes. They issue a prospectus representing that they had agreed to purchase the property for a sum largely in excess of the amount which they had, in fact, to pay. On the faith of this prospectus they collect subscriptions from a confiding and credulous public. And then comes the last act. Secretly, and therefore dishonestly, they put into their own pockets the difference between the real and the pretended price. After a brief career the company is ordered to be wound up. In the course of the liquidation the trick is discovered. Mr Gluckstein is called upon to make good a portion of the sum which he and his associates had misappropriated. Why Mr Gluckstein alone was selected for attack I do not know any more than I know why he was only asked to pay back a fraction of the money improperly withdrawn from the coffers of the company. . . . In this matter Mr Gluckstein has been in my opinion extremely fortunate. But he complains that he may have difficulty in recovering from his co-directors their share of the spoil, and he asks that the official liquidator may proceed against his associates before calling upon him to make good the whole amount with which he has been charged. My Lords, there may be occasions in which that would be a proper course to take. But I cannot think that this is a case in which any indulgence ought to be shown to Mr Gluckstein. He may or may not be able to recover a contribution from those who joined with him in defrauding the company. He can bring an action at law if he likes. If he hesitates to take that course or takes it and fails, then his only remedy lies in an appeal to that sense of honour which is popularly supposed to exist among robbers of a humbler type.

Well! I think that is a perfect piece of plain, *expository*, English—with a shrewd sting in its tail.

So far, my quotations have been examples of English put to polemical, narrative, descriptive, and expository purposes. My next two specimens of Good English strike a deeper note: they verge, both of them, upon the philosophical, though neither is the work of a professed philosopher: one of them was written by a statesman, the other by a scholar.

And this is perhaps an appropriate moment to point out that I have been keeping a strict chronological order in the pieces of prose that I have brought to your attention, and that by now we are well on the way into the twentieth century.

Here, then is my first example of what I will call good *reflective* English:

Man, so far as natural science by itself is able to teach us, is no longer the final cause of the Universe, the Heaven-descended heir of all the ages. His very existence is an accident, his story a brief and transitory episode in the life of one of the meanest of the planets. Of the combination of causes which first converted a dead organic compound into the living progenitors of humanity, science, indeed, as yet knows nothing. It is enough that from such beginnings, famine, disease, and mutual slaughter, fit nurses of the future lords of creation, have gradually evolved, after infinite travail, a race with conscience enough to feel that it is vile, and intelligence enough to know that it is insignificant. We survey the past, and see that its history is of blood and tears, of helpless blundering, of wild revolt, of stupid acquiescence, of empty aspirations. We sound the future, and learn that after a period, long compared with the individual life, but short indeed compared with the divisions of time open to our investigation, the energies of our system will decay, the glory of the sun will be dimmed, and the earth, tideless and inert, will no longer tolerate the race which has for a moment disturbed its solitude. Man will go down into the pit, and all his thoughts will perish. The uneasy consciousness, which in this obscure corner has for a brief space broken the contented silence of the universe, will be at rest. Matter will know itself no longer. 'Imperishable monuments' and 'immortal deeds', death itself, and love, stronger than death, will be as though they had never been. Nor will anything that is be better or worse for all that the labour, genius, devotion and suffering of man have striven through countless generations to effect.

That comes from A. J. Balfour's *Foundations of Belief*. It is, surely, an eloquent passage—none the less eloquent for being, as it is, a *tour de force*: for Mr Balfour, though a defender of philosophic doubt, was himself a convinced believer in personal immortality, and he is here acting the part of *advocatus diaboli*, stating his opponents's case—surely with a dangerously persuasive power?

I follow this with a passage containing the confession of faith—or, rather, lack of faith—of a thorough-going sceptic, Gilbert Murray, who still occupied the Chair of Greek at Oxford when I was an undergraduate. Murray raises the same issue as Arthur Balfour, and describes simply and sincerely his attitude towards the supernatural; it comes from an early work of his—*Five Stages of Greek Religion*:

I confess it seems strange to me as I write here, to reflect that at this moment many of my friends and most of my fellow-creatures are, as far as one can judge, quite confident that they possess super-natural knowledge. As a rule, each individual belongs to some body which has received in writing the results of a divine revelation. I cannot share in any such feeling. The uncharted surrounds us on every side and we must needs have some relation to it, a relation which will depend on the general discipline of a man's mind and the bias of his whole character. As far as knowledge and conscious reason will go, we should follow resolutely their austere guidance. When they cease, as cease they must, we must use as best we can those fainter powers of apprehension and surmise and sensitiveness by which, after all, most high truth has been reached as well as most high art and poetry; careful always really to seek for truth and not for our own emotional satisfaction, careful not to neglect the real needs of men and women through basing our life on dreams; and remembering above all to walk gently in a world where the lights are dim and the very stars wander.

My last example is the work of a master of the English language, who has used it, surely, to greater effect—I am thinking of his addresses to the nation in the dark days of 1940—than any of his contemporaries. No one would cite those as examples of good English: they are something more than that. Let me quote another example of Winston Churchill's linguistic accomplishment— a *tour de force* quite unknown, I think, to most of his admirers. It is rather long, but it is very light, and I hope you will bear with me if I read it to the end. It takes the unpromising form of a letter to *The Times*:

Sir,

Observing reports in various newspapers that prayers are about to be offered up for rain in order that the present serious drought may be terminated, I venture to suggest that great care should be taken in framing the appeal.

On the last occasion when this extreme step was resorted to, the Duke of Rutland took the leading part with so much well-meaning enthusiasm that the resulting downpour was not only sufficient for all immediate needs, but was considerably in excess of what was actually required, with the consequence that the agricultural community had no sooner been delivered from the drought than they were clamouring for a special interposition to relieve them from the deluge.

Profiting by this experience, we ought surely on this occasion to be extremely careful to state exactly what we want in precise terms, so as to obviate the possibility of any misunderstanding, and to economize so far as possible the need for these special appeals. After so many days of drought, it certainly does not seem unreasonable to ask for a change in the weather, and faith in a favourable response may well be fortified by actuarial probabilities.

While therefore welcoming the suggestion that His Grace should again come forward, I cannot help feeling that the Board of Agriculture should first of all be consulted. They should draw up a schedule of the exact amount of rainfall required in the interests of this year's harvest in the different parts of the country. This schedule should be placarded in the various places of worship at the time when the appeal is made. It would no doubt be unnecessary to read out the whole schedule during the service, so long as it was made clear at the time that this is what we have in our minds, and what we actually want at this juncture.

I feel sure that this would be a much more businesslike manner of dealing with the emergency than mere vague appeals for rain. But, after all, even this scheme, though greatly preferable to the haphazard methods previously employed, is in itself only a partial makeshift. What we really require to pray for is the general amelioration of the British climate. What is the use of having these piecemeal interpositions—now asking for sunshine, now for rain? Would it not be far better to ascertain by scientific investigation, conducted under the auspices of a Royal Commission, what is the proportion of sunshine and rain best suited to the ripening of the British crops? It would no doubt be necessary that other interests besides agriculture should be represented, but there must be certain broad general reforms in the British weather upon which an overwhelming consensus of opinion could be found. The proper proportion of rain to sunshine during each period of the year; the relegation of the rain largely to the hours of darkness; the apportionment of rain and sunshine as between different months, with proper reference not only to crops but to holidays; all these could receive due consideration. A really scientific basis of climatic reform would be achieved.

These reforms, when duly embodied in an official volume, could be made the object of the sustained appeals of the nation over many years, and embodied in general prayers of a permanent and not of an exceptional character. We should not then be forced from time to time to have recourse to such appeals at particular periods, which, since they are unrelated to any general plan, must run the risk of deranging the whole economy of nature, and involve the interruption and deflection of universal processes, causing reactions of the utmost complexity in many directions which it is impossible for us with our limited knowledge to foresee.

I urge you, Sir to lend the weight of your powerful organ to the systematization of our appeals for the reform of the British climate.

Yours very faithfully,
SCORPIO

Well! as I have said, I think that is a piece of English that could only have been written by a master of the language, and I hope you will not think it too light a note on which to conclude this rapid, but I trust not altogether superficial, survey of an almost uncharted territory—the realm of Good English.

Public Notices

Ever since, as a child, I learned to read, I have been fascinated by the printed word. I don't mean simply that I have always loved reading books. Of course, I love reading books; but my love of reading isn't confined to the printed page. I am fascinated by the visible word, whether in manuscript or in print, wherever I find it. When I walked about the streets as a boy, my eye was continually engaged by the display of words on hoardings, on notice boards, on shop-fronts, on omnibuses. And it is the same now I am grown up. Even when I'm driving a car, and it isn't really practicable to study notices other than traffic signs, I can't resist the challenge offered by the registration numbers on the cars of other motorists. They always (or almost always) begin with three letters, and those letters provide me with verbal material: they must somehow, I feel, be made into a word. Sometimes I actually forbid myself to overtake the car in front of me until, out of the three letters on its number plate, I have made up the name of a well-known person. My rule is, you can add any number of letters, but you mustn't alter the order of the three

given letters. The other day, for instance I passed
two cars in quick succession. YBW were the letters on the first number-plate: not very difficult!—
STANLEY BALDWIN. The next was easier still:
LRX (that's quite common on the number-plates
of cars in Oxfordshire). Well, I supplied KAR
before the L, and MA between the L and the RX,
and the second car also was overtaken.

Car registration numbers, however, though
they may provide tempting material for the word-
addict on the public highway, aren't really public
notices. What about advertisements? Well, they
are public notices in a sense; but they are notices
of a special kind, and they deserve a study to
themselves. They don't just state a fact, like 'PRI-
VATE ROAD'; or issue a command, like 'DRIVE
SLOWLY', or give a warning, like 'TRESPASSERS
WILL BE PROSECUTED' (I'll have more to say
about that notice later on).

I rule out also *graffiti*. They too are public
notices, of a kind—a strange mixture, most of
them, of the public and the personal. Sometimes,
of course, they are merely obscene—just drunken
scrawls; sometimes, on the other hand, they give
expression to a sort of protest: the common note is
hostility to the conventional, the respectable. I
remember in the days of student unrest, ten years
ago, there appeared on the walls of Oxford *graffiti*
intended to give expression to the ideals of the

youthful revolutionists, for instance, WHAT DO WE WANT? EVERYTHING. WHEN DO WE WANT IT? NOW! That was one. Another conveyed an exhortation—more modest in its demands but equally unpractical: SMASH HYPOCRISY NOW. Well, fortunately they didn't bring it off, and hypocrisy—I don't mean Pecksniffian humbug, I mean the pretences, the false appearances, that are kept up by decent people for reasons of mutual consideration and forbearance—that kind of hypocrisy remains, as it has always been, a cement that holds together civilized society.

Passing over advertisements, then, and *graffiti*, I shall concentrate on official notices, posted, usually by persons in authority, in order to provide information, or to convey a warning, or to promulgate an order, to the general public. Often these notices reflect current social conditions and fashions, in the language they use, the matters they deal with, and the messages they convey.

Let me start with a homely example. Fifty or more years ago you would see, posted in the streets and squares of any sizeable town, notices bearing the legend EXPECTORATION PROHIBITED. 'Expectoration'! If that notice were posted up today, many people wouldn't know what it was that was being forbidden. That old-fashioned injunction was long ago superseded by the short, sharp, command DO NOT SPIT—a very familiar notice in my young days. Even that has gone out now; the prohibition isn't required: people, on the whole, don't spit anymore. The public notice, in this minor matter, is an indication of social progress, of a change in the habits of the people.

Then, take the very familiar notices posted outside public lavatories: GENTLEMEN (it used to be) over one door, LADIES over the other. Nowadays (I suppose because 'Gentlemen' and 'Ladies' suggests an unacceptable class-distinction) it is usually MEN and WOMEN—and those words are now themselves giving way to a pictorial notice—a trousered figure over one door, and a skirted figure over the other. (Even this pictorial notice has become old-fashioned and has its dangers: it doesn't mean exactly what it—well! I can't say 'what it says'—it doesn't mean what it depicts: a girl wearing trousers would be mistaken if she took it literally—if 'literally' is the right word where a picture is concerned).

I don't want to linger too long in the precincts of the public lavatory, but I can't help recalling a notice which confronted every male visitor to a public lavatory as he made his exit: GENTLEMEN ARE KINDLY REQUESTED TO ADJUST THEIR DRESS BEFORE LEAVING—in other words: 'Don't forget to do up your fly-buttons'. That dignified reminder has practically disappeared from the English scene: but I am told that in America you may come upon its modern counterpart: XYZ—'EXamine Your Zip.'

So much for notices that reflect changes in the habits of the society whose members they are addressed to. Let me now indulge what I have called my addiction to words, and invite you to consider public notices, as it were, æsthetically; to judge them as a quasi-literary form. Perhaps I ought to say 'prose' form. Poetry they certainly are not—though I must tell you that I thought I detected a poetic echo in a public notice which I saw only the other day posted in the hedge close by a farm-yard gate, as a warning to passing motorists. It was just four words long: TRACTOR, it proclaimed, and then underneath, TRACTOR TURNING RIGHT. 'Tractor,' I repeated to myself, 'Tractor, tractor, turning right.' The farmer who put up that notice, had he been reading Blake? And I found it hard to restrain myself from supplementing that practical prose notice with a poetical graffito:

> Tractor, tractor, turning right
> In the forests of the night . . .

Well, that's just a bit of fantasy. A poetical public notice is really a contradiction in terms. The medium such notices are composed in is prose of a kind. But they are by no means easy to compose. They should be short, or as short as possible—

without a superfluous word. Their text must be suitable to be presented in capital letters and without the aid of punctuation; complicated subordinate clauses are out of the question. Above all, they must avoid ambiguity, telling the reader what it is that he must do, or what it is that he may not do; and if they are minatory or cautionary notices, they must make plain what he is being warned against, and what he ought to do to avoid the threatened danger.

Here is a good example of a notice that, in my opinion, does not stand up to that test. I saw it only the other day in the Strangers' Gallery in the House of Lords: *Demonstrations by Strangers in the Gallery are out of order and must be treated accordingly*. Well, one gets the general drift: 'No demonstrations!' But what about 'must be treated accordingly'?' 'Must be'? Who is being addressed? Who is it who's to treat the demonstrators (or the demonstrations) 'accordingly', and what on earth does 'accordingly' mean? I only wonder that the author of that notice didn't add the words BY ORDER—which are often subjoined to mandatory notices because they are supposed to increase the impressiveness of the message, though in fact they mean nothing at all.

And that reminds me of TRESPASSERS WILL BE PROSECUTED—probably of all public notices the one that is most familiar to people who have spent any of their time walking in the country-side. Here again the intention of the message in plain: 'Keep Out!', it means, 'This is private property'. But the explicit threat contained in the message is an empty one; the notice-board carrying it—to quote the words of a Victorian judge—is no more than 'a wooden lie'. Trespassing is not in itself a criminal offence and does not of itself render the trespasser liable to prosecution. The notice is displayed simply *in terrorem* —to frighten people off. And it must be confessed that if it were altered so as to present an accurate statement of the law and if it ran: 'Trespassers may render themselves liable to a civil action for damages and (if they persist in their trespass) to an action for an injunction,' that would—to put it mildly—diminish its effectiveness.

Then there's a notice that is to be seen on some moving staircases in the Underground: DOGS MUST BE CARRIED. What is one to do, one may ask, if one hasn't got a dog? Well, you'll tell me that I'm just being captious, that I know perfectly well what it means. I admit that I know what it's meant to mean, but that's not the point. An æsthetically satisfactory notice should say what it means, and say it unambiguously.

I am worried also by the little rubbish-bins that I see in railway-stations bearing the legend

FOR LITTER. That seems to me to be plainly self-contradictory. How can you obey the implied injunction? If you do put your empty cigarette-packet in the bin, then it isn't litter—and it is for litter, the inscription tells us, that the bin is provided. It must surely mean FOR WHAT WOULD (or MIGHT) BE LITTER IF YOU DON'T PUT IT IN HERE. But that breaks my first rule of notice-composition—it is hopelessly complicated and long-winded.

Sometimes the defect in a notice can be cured without altering the text, simply by re-arranging it. A friend reported to me the other day a road-side notice which said, in one long line, LOOSE STONES TRAVEL SLOWLY. Well, I dare say they do: rolling stones, we know, gather no moss. No doubt a colon after STONES, and an exclamation mark after SLOWLY, would have made the intended meaning plain; but punctuation is not allowed. The cure is surely to reverse the order: TRAVEL SLOWLY LOOSE STONES—and, better still, to set it out in two lines, with TRAVEL SLOWLY as the upper line and LOOSE STONES below it.

There's the same sort of ambiguity about the unpunctuated notices one sees outside filling stations: PETROL SNACKS don't sound to me very appetising, and as for PARKING TOILETS, imagination boggles at the idea. A little rearrangement of the text, putting the second word below the first, instead of after it, would remove the ambiguity. Another garage notice that is—shall I say—falsely suggestive, is one that I saw the other day advertising TIRES AND EXHAUSTS—and the impression of fatigue created by this advertisement was increased by the fact that tyres was spelt with an 'i' instead of a 'y'.

I said that the first aim of the composer of a public notice should be to avoid ambiguity. I am afraid that that aim is not always achieved. Warning notices, in particular, often leave me simply perplexed. Sometimes it's clear what it is that one's being warned against, but not clear what one's supposed to do about it; sometimes it is not even clear (to me, at any rate) what is the subject of the warning. DANGER FALLING ROCKS and BEWARE LOW-FLYING AIRCRAFT are both familiar roadside notices. The danger is plainly indicated; not so the remedy. The only comment I feel inclined to make, in each case, can be expressed by the colloquial phrase 'So what?'

To the other category, the *completely* bewildering caution, belong two notices I saw the other day, one a road-sign, the other placed on the wall beside a post-office. The first said DANGEROUS HAIRPIN; the second said WARNING CLEARANCE LIMITED. I think I can guess the sort of thing the first one is talking about—something,

I suppose, to do with a bend in the road; but the second leaves me completely mystified. It is placed, as I said, near the entrance to a post-office. Can it have anything to do with the frequency with which the letter-box is emptied? 'CLEAR-ANCE LIMITED': that might explain the postal delays which are an increasingly common feature of life to-day.

Now I must strike a more solemn note. The other day, in his column in the *Daily Telegraph*, the journalist Peterborough, I believe, called attention to a notice to be seen outside the premises of an Undertaker and Funeral Director: PARKING (it ran) PARKING RESERVED FOR REGULAR CUS-TOMERS—rather grim! But I can't help suggesting an improvement: wouldn't it have been even better if it had said PERMANENT PARKING RE-SERVED FOR REGULAR CUSTOMERS?

The same solemn note is struck by a notice which an old friend of mine reported to me years ago from the suburbs of North London: NO ROAD BEYOND THE CEMETERY *By Order of the Hendon Borough Council*. It sounds, doesn't it, as if the Council were claiming to be a more than local authority!

Let me now conclude my survey with two examples from what one might call the private sector: each was composed by a friend of mine (both of them—alas!—are dead) for display upon his

own property. Both of them are in a sense paro-
dies of an official notice; one of them, but not
the other, was meant to be taken seriously. The
first was a *jeu d'esprit*—I think that's the most
appropriate phrase—of Lord Berners. One of the
things he enjoyed doing was teasing people. He
lived in a beautiful house at Faringdon in Berk-
shire. At several points on the fence that ran
round his estate he posted a notice that could not
fail to attract the attention of the passer-by; it ran
DOGS WILL BE SHOT. CATS WILL BE WHIP-
PED. Any dog reading that warning might well
have been alarmed by its opening words; but
his alarm would surely have been allayed when
he saw what was to happen to the cats—like
TRESPASSERS WILL BE PROSECUTED, it was
an empty threat, only intended *in terrorem*.

My other private-public notice is one that was
posted by Evelyn Waugh on the gate-way of his
house in the country, where he would retire to see
his friends, and write his novels, he hoped, in
peace. Its legend was very simple:

NO ADMITTANCE ON BUSINESS

I think that that fulfils perfectly the rules I suggested for composing an effective public notice:
the text is brief and its meaning is unambiguous—
no one who read those words could have had any
doubt about what they meant, or about how to
comply with the message they conveyed.

Growing Old

I want to talk about Growing Old because it's something I think about a good deal nowadays; and I think about it because I'm just beginning to do it myself. I suppose you might say that we're all of us doing it (I mean, growing old) every day of our lives; at least, we're all, even infants in their cradles, growing *older* every day, though we may never live to be what most people would call *old*. There is a sort of paradox here, a verbal ambiguity, like the ambiguity involved in saying of an invalid, 'He's better, but he's not really *well* yet.' How can you be *better* if you're not even *well*? How can you grow *older* if you're not yet *old*?

You may think that this is just playing with words; but the word-play conceals, or expresses, a point of substance, a real difficulty. Even the youngest living creature is old in one sense: Blake's Joy, you may remember, was 'but two days old'; Wordsworth's little cottage girl 'was eight years old', she said. But the word 'old' has a special meaning: 'that has lived long, advanced in years', is the dictionary definition. At a certain age—or, rather, at an *un*certain age—we begin to rank as 'old people'. 'I have been young and now am old', says the Psalmist: 'old' means 'no longer young'—indeed, 'no longer young' is a euphemism we sometimes employ—particularly if we are talking about what used to be called 'the weaker sex'—when we want to avoid the dread monosyllable, with all its positive implications.

Of course, the line that divides youth from age is a very wavy, uncertain one; and so are the boundaries that mark off all the subdivisions of our life—the boundaries that divide infancy from boyhood, boyhood from young manhood, young manhood from middle age, the middle-aged from the elderly (that's an interesting word; it seems to imply something more than a time of life; it suggests *respectability*: you can be an elderly gentleman, but who ever heard of an elderly savage?); then, after elderliness, comes old age; which, if you live long enough, turns into senility; then, if you live too long, comes second-childhood—and the circle, the sad circle, is complete.

There are two phrases, or forms of words, both of which crop up pretty frequently in common speech, and represent (so to speak) two ways of looking at old age—the absolute and the relative, one might call them. 'Be your age!' is the first, 'A man is as old as he feels' is the second. I've never been sure just what's meant by 'Be your age!' I suppose it's usually addressed to people who, though they've grown up, are behaving childishly or in a juvenile fashion; but whatever application it may have, the injunction 'Be your age!' assumes, first, that one has a real age, determined by the date of one's birth, and second, that one should accept that fact: 'Don't behave as if you were younger than you really are.' Those very reasonable assumptions are explicitly denied by the assertion that a man is as old as he feels. What that asserts is just the plain opposite of the truth: it assumes, quite rightly, that some people don't feel as old as they really are, and it encourages them to disregard their real age. It's just a piece of foolish optimism—like telling people who are concerned about their health that they're as well as they feel.

Well! I am afraid that I myself am beginning to be old in the absolute sense, judging simply by the length of time that has elapsed since I was born. 'The days of our age are three score years and ten', declares the Psalmist, and he goes on to say that though some men 'be so strong that they come to four score years, yet is their strength then but labour and sorrow'. No doubt the expectation of life is greater in Britain today than it was in Palestine in the days of the Psalmist; one has a better chance today of reaching eighty and of still being hale and hearty, or at least being in pretty good health. But, having reached three-score

years and ten, I suppose I must admit that I am—
how shall I put it? well!—no longer young. But I
don't *feel* old. I don't think of myself as an 'old
man'—the very idea that I should be so described
seems to me ridiculous. I hope I'm not one of
those dreadful old people I referred to a moment
ago, who refuse to 'be their age', and cultivate a
boyish, juvenile, manner just in order to show
that they're not becoming senile—or to conceal
the fact that they *are* becoming senile. In fact, I
know I don't do that. It's just that, as I say, I don't
feel old. But the fact that I have lived a large number of years is borne in upon me in several ways.
Some of these reminders are internal (so to
speak)—changes in my own body or my mind—
and some of them are external.

First, the internal. Of course my faculties, my
physical faculties, aren't what they were. I don't
play outdoor games—at least, none more stre-
nuous than croquet; I don't go for long country
walks; and I have to wear spectacles for reading.
But all these disabilities began to affect me years
ago, in early middle age. I don't think I'm any
lazier than I used to be, but I fall asleep more
readily—in an easy chair after lunch, or in any
kind of chair after dinner. Then there's the question of my hair. I've been lucky (or at least, I
suppose I should count myself lucky) in keeping a
full complement of hair upon my head. But it's

69

changing its colour. Not so much on the top of my head—the change there is hardly, as yet, perceptible. But, my eyebrows! On many mornings, I spend five or ten minutes in front of the looking-glass on my dressing-table, snipping off with my nail-scissors the white hairs that are beginning to invade them, in ever increasing numbers. Vanity on my part, you say? I don't think it's vanity; I'd do it just the same if I were living alone on a desert island. (But perhaps you'll say it's the extreme of vanity, to care about your eyebrows when you're living alone on a desert island . . .) I think that really it's just a sense of decency, a liking for order and tidiness and a dislike of change.

But of course the most distressing symptom of old age is the loss, or impairment, of one's memory. I won't dilate upon that: it happens to almost everyone at my time of life, and there's nothing one can do about it. But there's one thing I've noticed about my own loss of memory that I find rather alarming. I don't think it's just my memory that's failing. I think it's my mind, or one of my mental faculties.

Memory is a word with a double meaning: it means a storehouse, in our mind, of facts and impressions; and it also means the power of recalling those facts and impressions and identifying them. 'Losing one's memory' means losing that power of recall. Well! I am losing the power of recall: I don't remember things that belong to the distant past. But, worse than that, I can't remember what happened yesterday. And I don't think that's due to a failure of the power of recalling things stored in my memory: I think that these recent happenings don't get stored away at all— and that's not because my memory contains so much that there's no room for more, but because my mind simply doesn't register things as they happen. I think (I hope I'm not deceiving myself!) that my power of understanding things and reasoning about them, my intellect, such as it is, is no better and no worse than it has always been; but the simple gift of consigning things to memory seems to be disappearing.

So much for what I have called the *internal* symptoms of age. Now for the external symptoms—I mean, the changes or happenings in the outside world that remind me that I am—well!— older than I was. First, let me mention an entirely acceptable reminder. Besides qualifying for what is bluntly called an Old Age Pension, I rejoice, whenever I travel by train or take a bus in Oxford, (which is where I live) in the benefits accorded by British Rail, and by the local bus service, to what they call a Senior Citizen—a euphemistic title invented, presumably, by a Civil Servant—I must say, a very civil Civil Servant—to describe old people like myself. It isn't clear to me (by the way)

71

why older people should pay less on trains and buses than their juniors. Surely they're lucky not to have to pay *more*? Old people, after all, travel mainly for pleasure; and, if they have been thrifty during their long lives, they can afford the fare better than young people, who may have a family to support and may have to travel to work every day. Why shouldn't Senior Citizens' tickets cost not half as much, but twice as much as the ordinary working man's? I just throw out the suggestion, the very logical suggestion, to the Chancellor of the Exchequer (or should it be the Minister of Transport?) in case he wants to lose a large number of votes (mine, I must say, would be among them) at the next General Election.

But let me be serious, if only for a moment. The most distressing reminder of my own advancing age—and it's a reminder that recurs (alas) more and more frequently as the years, or even as the months, go by—is the news that a friend of mine has died. It was bad enough when *The Times* appeared daily, and all too often contained a notice of the death of a friend or an acquaintance—many of them, I may say, no older than myself. But now the first news of somebody's death may be the casual mention by a friend: 'Oh! didn't you know? Poor X died a couple of months ago!' And here my failing memory plays its part: often, I can't remember whether so-and-so—of course, I'm thinking now not of close friends, but of a wider circle of acquaintances—I can't remember whether so-and-so, whom I haven't seen for years, is alive or dead.

And there's another thing, connected with the passage of time as it affects my friends (or is it myself that is affected?): all my contemporaries, or near-contemporaries, seem to grow older much more quickly nowadays. 'How old is Tomkins?' I am asked. 'He must be getting on for fifty,' I reply—and it turns out that he's sixty-three. 'Add fifteen to the number you first thought of' is the rule I have learned to apply in such cases.

Of course, the deaths of one's contemporaries remind one not only that one is growing old, but also that the older one grows, the nearer one gets to the day when one will have to die oneself. Gibbon faces this prospect in a passage at the end of his *Memoirs*, which were written in 1789, soon after he had completed *The Decline and Fall*. He was then fifty-two years old. 'The present,' he says, 'is a fleeting moment, the past is no more; and our prospect of futurity is dark and doubtful. This day,' he continues, 'may possibly be my last; but the laws of probability, so true in general, so fallacious in particular, still allow about fifteen years.' When he wrote those words, Gibbon had, in fact, only five more years to live. Today, when

73

one gets past seventy, as I have done, one is living on borrowed time.

Let me make it plain that I don't want to die. About the possibility of an after-life, I wouldn't be dogmatic: I suppose I'd call myself an agnostic. But I must say that I've never for a moment believed that we somehow go on living after our bodily death. And I don't know whether if I did believe in an after-life, that would reconcile me to 'departing' *this* life. Anyhow, I am by no means ready to die yet. And I don't think much about my death; I put off making my will, not because I shrink from the idea of it, or because I can't face making the decisions it would involve, but simply out of procrastination—it's easier to put things off. And my habit of procrastination gets worse as I get older: the less time I have left to do things in, the longer I put off doing them. I'm not proud of this—but I'm not as ashamed of it as I ought to be—indeed, I have recorded this failing of mine in half-a-dozen lines of verse:

> Here, with his talents in a napkin hid,
> Lies one who much designed, and nothing did:
> Postponing and deferring, day by day
> He quite procrastinated life away,
> And when at length the summons came to die
> With his last breath put off—mortality.

I don't feel that death is imminent: I don't feel the

force of the poet's injunction: 'Look thy last on all things lovely.' But I do find myself saying sometimes half-regretfully as I look at my belongings: 'That hair-brush will see me through, I suppose. I'll never buy another dressing-gown—or (I suspect) another pair of bedroom slippers.' And I find that I take an ever-increasing pleasure in my possessions, my pictures and my books (book-collecting has been a life-long passion of mine). I'm more self-sufficient, less interested in the outside world. People in the street seem to me to be uglier, more vulgar, more dreadful, than they used to be. Is the change in me, I wonder, or in them?

Then, I find that I take immense pleasure in the company of children—a thing I never used to do. Why is this? It's not mere sentimentality—'dear little things!', that sort of thing. They have to be nice, intelligent and good-looking children if I am to like them, and of course, I want them to like *me* too. Is this really due to a change in myself, brought about by my advancing years? I incline to think that it's just because I've now more time to spend with them—I never really *noticed* children before. In one respect, old age adds—shall I say?— *poignancy* to this relationship: I often wonder what my very young friends will be like when they've grown up—and I have to accept the fact that I shall never know.

Well! I've taken up all this talk with an

account—a very patchy and superficial account—
of my own experience, of my feelings and reflections on the process of growing old. Perhaps the
time would have been more profitably spent if I
had offered an anthology of what the poets and
the philosophers have had to say about old age—
from the dreadful sentimental cheeriness of
Browning's *Rabbi Ben Ezra*—'Grow old along with
me! the best is yet to be'—to Matthew Arnold's
splendid and devastating poem, *Growing Old*—

> What is it to grow old? . . .
> It is to spend long days
> And not once feel that we were ever young . . .
> Deep in our hidden heart
> Festers the dull remembrance of a change,
> But no emotion—none.

I could have provided a rich feast from the poets.
As for the philosophers, I have dipped into a few
of the sages who have discussed old age, from
Cicero onwards, but I can't say that I have learned
very much from them. They seem to agree that
old age is the happiest period of a man's life,
provided that he is equipped with two essentials—first, *virtue*, and the consciousness of a life
well spent; second, *ample pecuniary resources*. Gibbon, in the concluding paragraphs of his *Memoirs*,
from which I have already quoted, sums it up
well. 'The first and indispensable requisite of happiness,' he declares, 'is a clear conscience, unsul-
76

lied by the reproach or remembrance of an unworthy action.' Gibbon doesn't go so far as to lay claim to that—nor, indeed, do I. But he doesn't suffer from pangs of conscience or remorse: 'Some mischievous appetites and habits,' he says, 'have perhaps been corrected by philosophy or time.' I hope I would be justified in making the same modest claim. But the satisfactions of a clear conscience, as Gibbon very frankly says, 'would be tasteless or bitter if their possession were not assured by an annual and adequate supply.' And in this respect, he continues, 'I am indeed rich, since my income is equal to my expense and my expense is equal to my riches.' Well! I can't call myself rich; but on this point I can 'say ditto to Mr. Gibbon': I've nothing to complain about. But, like Gibbon, I don't find a reasonably clear conscience and a reasonably adequate income, though they are necessary prerequisites, I don't find them a sufficient guarantee of happiness.

The historian and philosopher Fontenelle said that old age was the most agreeable period of his long life— and he lived to be only a few days short of a hundred. 'I am far more inclined,' says Gibbon, 'to embrace than to dispute this comfortable doctrine. . . . But I must reluctantly observe that two causes, the abbreviation of time, and the failure of hope, will always tinge with a browner shade the evening of life.'

Memory

I want to talk about memory—memory and the loss of memory—about remembering and forgetting. That is a subject that has been in my mind a good deal during the last year or two. I have got to the time of life when people say to one: 'I see you've reached retiring age. What are you going to do in your retirement? Have you thought of writing your Recollections?'—or else, 'I suppose you're going to give us your Memoirs? What a lot of interesting people you must have met!'

Well! When people say that to me, I tell them that I have at least one excellent reason (there are others) for not writing my Memoirs, and that is that I am losing my memory—which wasn't a very good one at the best of times—and if you can't remember anything, that's rather a disqualification for writing Recollections, or at any rate for writing truthful ones.

I said that I never had a very good memory. What does one mean when one talks about a 'good memory'? There are several sorts of good memory, none of which I myself am blessed with.

First, an *efficient* memory: 'He's a marvellous secretary—never forgets a thing. Never fails to bring a relevant point before the Committee. I don't know what we'd do without him.' That's not really having a good memory; it's making the best use of what may be a perfectly ordinary one.

Then, second, there's a *remarkable* memory, like Macaulay's, who could repeat word for word a newspaper article, as soon as he had finished reading it.

Third, a *retentive* memory like—well, I can't remember who it was! Anyway, someone who knew *Paradise Lost* by heart, and, if you chose a line at random, could recite the text, without hesitation, from that point to the end of the poem.

Fourth, there's what one might call a *long-distance* memory—the ability to recall events or experiences from the very distant past. Dr Samuel Parr, who died in 1825 at the age of 78, claimed to his dying day that he remembered being suckled at his mother's breast. Of course, there was no means of checking this; one had to take his word for it. There are people whose memories enable them to form a link, so to speak, in a chain that spans the centuries—the kind of people who said to one in the nursery 'Take a good look at me and don't forget me: when you grow up you can tell your grand-children you met a man who attended the coronation of Queen Victoria.'

Such claims should always be tested carefully. I recall two stories about men who remembered setting eyes on Napoleon.

The first was an old Russian peasant who claimed that as a child he saw Napoleon when, in 1812, the Emperor passed through his village during the retreat from Moscow. Eighty or ninety years later, the Tsar happened to be in the neighbourhood, and heard the story. His interest was keenly aroused, and he had the old man brought before him, and plied him with questions. 'Is it true that you remember Napoleon passing through your village when you were a child?' 'Yes Sire' said the peasant, 'He rode through the village at the head of his staff.' 'But did you actually set eyes on the Emperor himself?' 'Yes Sire, indeed I did.' 'Do you remember what he looked like?' 'Yes, I remember very well, he had a long white beard.' The Tsar was not pleased; and the unfortunate peasant had to be hustled hastily away.

What was the explanation? Of course the old man wasn't trying to deceive the Tsar; he was telling him truthfully what he remembered—or what he thought he remembered. Was it that his memory—as memory is said to do sometimes—was playing him tricks? Had he subconsciously manufactured an image, a 'recollection', that had no counterpart in his actual experience?

I think that the explanation must have been a more innocent one than that. The fault did not lie in his memory any more than it lay in his veracity: his memory recorded accurately what, at the time, he thought it was that he perceived. Picture him, as an infant—a tiny child by the roadside, looking up at the Emperor riding by on his grey charger Marengo—the scene is recorded in a famous painting by Meissonnier. May it not have been that, as the procession passed by, Marengo's flowing white tail obscured his view and coalesced in his child's eye with the image of the Emperor himself, and that for ever after he re-membered what he thought he saw?

The second story is from nearer home. One of the last Life Fellows of my old Oxford college, All Souls, was the Honourable Edmund Bertie, who was born in 1800 and died in 1886. As a boy Bertie had seen the Bellerophon moored at Torbay on its way to St Helena. He was very willing, as an old man, to recall the scene—a scene now familiar to many through Orchardson's well-known picture: the solitary figure on the deck, plunged in thought, in recollection, it may be, of his past triumphs, or anticipation of his years of exile.

When Bertie was an old man, junior Fellows of All Souls—men whom I knew in college, forty or fifty years later—would egg him on, in the Com-mon Room after dinner, to give his recollections of the scene, well knowing what it was that they were going to get from him. They would ply him with questions, pretending never to have heard the story before. (It is common knowledge, by the way, that memory is, so to speak, selective: people will remember a story, but won't remember how often they have told it you). The young men would lead him on, to their culminating question: 'Tell us, Bertie, can you sum up the impression that the Emperor left upon you?' The answer never varied, and it was contained in a single sentence: 'You could tell at once that he was NOT a University man.' A more accurate impression, no doubt, than that of the Russian peasant—but scarcely more informative. Indeed, the story illustrates the truth that people's recollections often tell you more about the recollector himself than about what it was that he remembered.

As I said at the beginning of this talk, it's forgetting as well as remembering that I'm concerned with—not only memory, but loss of memory. My own memory was never a good one, but, such as it is, or was, I'm beginning to lose it, and I find this both a worrying and an interesting process.

What do people say when I tell them that I'm losing my memory—which I often have to do—in order to explain why I've forgotten their name, or forgotten where it was that last we met? Well, the pattern of the ensuing dialogue is almost in-variable: 'Oh! I don't wonder you forget names; you must meet so many people!' To which I reply 'As a matter of fact, I live rather out of the world nowadays, and don't meet half as many people as I used to do!' Then they try to put me at my ease: 'Oh!', they say, 'I do it myself: I'm always forget-ting people's names and faces.' To which, if I am in an honest mood, I reply 'I don't believe you. And it would be no comfort to me if I did; my own worry is that my memory is getting worse and worse.' Then they say 'But don't you find that, though you may forget recent things, things from the past come back to you more clearly than they used to do?' That is, I think, a sentimental delusion. For my part, I can only say that my lack of memory extends, with complete impartiality, over the immediate past, the distant past, and the intervening years.

What do I forget? Well! I won't say 'everything': of course, that would be going too far. I am not in the championship class, like Lord William Cecil, the Bishop of Exeter, not many years ago, who used to travel about his diocese by train, and was on one occasion unable to produce his ticket to the inspector. 'Never mind! my Lord,' said the man; 'we all know you on this line.' 'That's all right for you', replied the Bishop, 'but what about me? Without my ticket, how can I tell where I'm going?' On such occasions he was reduced to telephoning home from the station and appealing to his wife or secretary to supply the necessary information—like G. K. Chesterton, who, in a similar plight, sent his wife the classic telegram: 'Am in Market Harborough. Where ought I to be?' As I say, I'm not in that class; but I've got a pretty good all-round lack of memory—words, facts, dates, names, and faces, I can forget them all. And I quite often have the trying experience of forgetting what it is that I've forgotten: 'There was something this morning that I was trying to remember—something important. What on earth was it?' Whatever it was, it is buried under a double layer of oblivion.

Then, appointments and engagements. 'Put them down', you'll say, 'in a little book!' Of course I do (if I remember to). But then, I forget where I have put the book—and, when I've found it, I all too often forget what the entry means: '3.00 p.m: W. G. *Important*'. 'Important', I'm sure it was: but who is 'W.G?'

And then, Christmas! Among the shower of Christmas cards that descend upon me, there are always several by which I am completely baffled: 'With best wishes and love as always—Jeremy and Gillian.' Jeremy and Gillian! Who are they? Old friends, evidently, and dear ones. But who? I look at the envelope, hoping that the postmark will provide a clue. 'Post early for Christmas' is all that I can decipher.

When I look through my address-book, which goes back thirty years or more, it provides me with similar experiences: it is crowded with names that bring back old memories, interspersed with names (complete with addresses) that bring back (alas!) no memories at all. Of course, I went to the Doctor about it. He prescribed some little pills: 'Take four of these each day, they may help.' They didn't do any good—but they never really had a fair trial, because I always forgot to take them.

Besides what I might call the sentimental disadvantages of a failing memory, there are the practical social embarrassments that arise from forgetting names and faces. 'I remember your face, but I'm afraid I've forgotten your name'— how often that represents the truth, but one wants to get by without having to say it! If you're going to say it, it's best to say it at the outset, or you may find yourself in an increasingly embarrassing situation, dreading the approach of a third party to whom you may have to introduce your interlocutor, with whom you have been chatting familiarly for ten minutes in the desperate, but unsuccessful, hope that you may recall his (or, worse still, her) name. To rescue yourself from such a situation, you have to be very dexterous, or very brazen. Dexterous or brazen, or both. That reminds me of one of the many stories about Dr Spooner, the legendary Warden of New College, Oxford, which tells how he went up to a junior colleague in the quadrangle and said to him 'Would you come to lunch with me next Sunday? I want you to meet our newly-elected Fellow, Stanley Casson.' 'But Mr Warden, I *am* Casson!' was the disconcerting reply. 'Never mind,' said Spooner, without a moment's hesitation, 'come all the same!' On another occasion—it must have been in the early 1920s, when a good many young men had returned from military service to finish their interrupted time at Oxford—the Warden is said to have put to an undergraduate the unexpected question: 'Tell me, was it you or your brother that was killed in the War?' There was, of course, no doubt about the answer: but it wasn't easy for the poor young man to know exactly how to put it.

Well! I must not be tempted into telling a string of anecdotes that belong to the borderland of memory—remembering, forgetting, mistaking, confusing, or simply being at a loss. And I must also resist the temptation— which is for me, I may say, a stronger one—to embark on the question *what memory is*: is remembering an intellectual, or (as Aristotle thought) a perceptual operation? And what exactly is it that we remember? Do we 'remember' actual things, events, facts, people?

Or do we 'remember' images of them that are somehow stored in our subconsciousness? And can you have a perceptual image of a fact? And how do you remember how to do things—how, for instance, to perform an arithmetical operation?

And what about forgetting? Can you forget anything unless it is actually there in your subconscious, ready to be forgotten? And if it is actually there, how is it possible for you to forget it?

There is matter here for at least another half-hour of philosophical or semi-philosophical enquiry. But I am forgetting (if that's the right word) how time flies; I must remember (if one can remember the present) that it's now time for me to stop.

Discrimination

I want to talk about a word, and about what that word stands for—about a word and a subject that crop up very frequently nowadays in every-day conversation and discussion and argument. I want to talk about 'discrimination.'

'Discrimination': etymologically it's the same as 'discernment'; it means the ability to distinguish, or the act of distinguishing, between one thing and another, or one kind of thing and another. This power of discerning differences is a gift that characterizes an intelligent being—a gift that man possesses in greater measure than the animals and the higher animals in greater measure than the lower.

'Discrimination' is used also in a special sense as meaning the power of judging and evaluating differences in quality, not only knowing one thing from another, but also knowing the good from the bad and the better from the less good—and a disposition to prefer the better to the worse. If we say of somebody that he is 'a discriminating person' we imply that he knows 'what's what', and that he is a man of taste: we are, surely, expressing admiration or approval of him. Ability to discriminate is, one would think, an enviable gift, and its exercise ought to be encouraged. 'Indiscriminate' is, surely, a pejorative term, whether it is applied to (say) a massacre—'innocent and guilty alike'—or in matters of taste—'he seems quite indiscriminate in his choice of friends, or in his choice of furniture.' To be incapable of discriminating is to be lacking in sensitiveness and taste.

Why is it then that 'discrimination' has, in England today—at any rate where discrimination between human beings is concerned—has today become a dirty word? Why are we told that in many social contexts we ought not to discriminate—that we ought to disregard actual differences between people or kinds of people and behave as it those differences did not exist?

It is easy to say 'Oh, it's a manifestation of the democratic feeling that is prevalent everywhere today, the craving for political and social equality, equality of status. The domination of wealth, the concept of a ruling class—those are things of the past.' I don't think that that's the explanation: it isn't a craving for political equality—one man, one vote—that's already been achieved; or for social equality, the abolition of class distinctions— class distinctions are surely on the way out. It is something much deeper than that. It is an increase in fellow-feeling among human beings, in our awareness of our common humanity. This deepening and widening of human feeling—I think it's noticeable particularly among intellectuals and among the younger generation—is due, I think, to a variety of causes. A number of things have combined, during the last fifty years or so, to make the world a smaller place than it used to be: most obviously, the 'media'—the wireless (as I can't help still calling it), which tells us every day what is actually happening in every quarter of the globe, and television, which brings distant places and things that are happening far away, before our very eyes. We are all living very close together nowadays: we are all in the same small boat.

And there is another way in which Science has quickened this sense of—if I may call it so—togetherness. Science, responsible for so many present-day amenities and conveniences—I won't beg a question and call them blessings—Science is responsible also for potential horrors and dangers of a kind, and of a magnitude, undreamed of a generation or so ago, dangers that today threaten us with universal extinction, or worse. We are all, indeed, in the same small boat, and we may well all go down in it together. Of course, the horrors nowadays threatened by war may make war itself less likely. All this—in the sphere of international relations—is common place, and I won't dwell upon it. What I want to emphasize is something that I think isn't generally appreciated—the humanizing effect that this combination of causes has had, without their realizing it, upon almost everyone who has to live in this small, heterogeneous, over-populated world.

Plainly, this deepening of the sense of human fellowship is a good thing. One wouldn't want to go against it. But may it not be carried—and may it not carry us—too far? It seems to me that an unrestrained insistence on the claims of our common humanity, on everyone's being treated alike, without regard to individual differences, may do more harm than good to society as a whole.

True, we are all equal before the law, whatever our race or creed or nationality, and irrespective of personal, individual, idiosyncrasies: if we break the law, we must answer for it, whoever and whatever we may be. The law, it is said, is no respecter of persons: that means that the Judge, in administering the law, and the jury, when deciding whether or not an accused person is guilty of a breach of it, must leave out of account, as irrelevant, the personal attributes of the accused (though, of course, some of these attributes may be taken into account by the Judge in deciding what is an appropriate sentence for a prisoner who has been found guilty). It does not mean that the substantive law—that is, the laws enacted by

Parliament and contained in the Statute Book—may not recognize differences between individuals and between categories of individual and impose different obligations upon them, even though the individual may have no control over, and no responsibility for, the attributes that render him liable to a legal obligation. The substantive law, the law that tells us what we may and may not do, is indeed a respecter of persons, and it is obviously right and necessary that it should be so. 'One law for the rich, and another for the poor,' people say. So there is, and quite right too—how else could one justify progressively higher rates of surtax on the higher 'income brackets'? The substantive law, the law by which our lives are regulated and our actions are controlled, must be a respecter of persons, and must discriminate between them. The problem presented by discrimination—when to discriminate between people, and what weight to attach to their differences—is a problem that faces not only legislators in framing laws, but ordinary people in the every day business of their lives. Every difference between one individual and another means a potential superiority and inferiority as between two of them: therefore, if you recognize their diversity and want to do justice to the individuals concerned, you may have to treat some people better than others. Discrimination implies recognition of the fact that some people, through no fault of their own, are inferior in gifts, in abilities, in character, to other people, and others, through no merit of their own, are superior. As a result of the increasingly strong feeling of human fellowship, of the weight to be attached to our common humanity—the causes of which I tried to analyse briefly at the beginning of this talk—discrimination, the recognition that some human beings are superior in character, ability, in attractive human qualities, has become a dirty word: people are reluctant to discriminate between two things or two people, because discriminating between them almost always means discriminating against one or other of them, and that goes against the humanitarian grain.

One area in which this anti-discriminatory tendency manifests itself very clearly is in the field of education, particularly in schools. In my school-days, a number of distinctions were very clearly drawn: distinctions between masters and boys, between the teachers and the taught, between games and work, between one subject and another—and (less clearly drawn, but no less important) between good boys and bad boys, the clever and the stupid, the industrious and the idle, and (a most important distinction, this!) between success and failure in examinations. These distinctions were clarified and emphasized by

93

school rules, by school discipline, and by the award of prizes and the imposition of punishments. Nowadays, it is not like that at all. Many school-masters, I think, and certainly many 'educationalists', allow their feeling for humanity, their shrinking from rigid discrimination, to carry them too far and too fast, to what seem to me to be regrettable extremes. I was looking the other day at the prospectus of a public school in which the new educational ideals were proudly expounded. Education, it said, is a joint enterprise, in which teacher and taught explore the world together, each party learning from the other. The idea of masters ('staff' is the word nowadays), the idea of masters teaching boys subjects was wholly wrong. The very conception of subjects was mischievous. 'Fragmentation', said the prospectus, was 'the great enemy': 'we try hard to break down the traditional barriers between areas and subjects' and to provide an 'Integrated Preparation for Life' (capital I, capital P, capital L).

One respect in which non-discrimination, the breaking down of old boundaries and distinctions, showed itself in the school I have just mentioned, is that it has become bi-sexual: it takes in girls as well as boys (indeed, it has among its houses a 'Girls International House'). This is happening all over the field of education, at schools and colleges alike. At Oxford, for instance, and

94

the same I believe is true of Cambridge, almost all the colleges have 'gone mixed', as they call it, the men's colleges taking in women and the women's colleges men. This involves, in every case, a change in the college statutes. At my own old college of All Souls, for instance, there is a clause—or rather there *was* a clause, until the college repealed it the other day—which said 'No woman shall become a member of the college.' The intention seems perfectly plain. But when I was Warden of the college I wondered what I would do if one of my colleagues presented himself to me one day and said 'Warden, I think I ought to warn you that I am spending the summer vacation at a clinic in Casablanca: when I return you must be prepared for a surprise.' And if I had said 'If that happens, you will have to resign your Fellowship,' he might have replied: 'Not so: the statute says that no woman may *become* a member of the college—not that no woman may *be* a member of the college. Nor does it say that no member of the college may become a woman.' Well, I'd have had no answer to that: I'm afraid I should have been nonplussed.

No-one can fail to be aware of the accelerated assimilation between the sexes that has been taking place during the past ten or twenty years. It isn't a question of women's rights or women's 'lib': it isn't sexual equality that is the goal aimed at: it is sexual indifference. Young people of either sex seem to want to camouflage their outward secondary characteristics, in order to emphasize their common humanity. It is most easily observable among the young, and it shows itself in their outward appearance—what they call their 'Lifestyle'. A generation ago, it used to be said, jokingly, that, what with women wearing trousers and men letting their hair grow long, you couldn't tell the boys from the girls when you met them in the street. What was said as a joke twenty years ago is the literal truth today. If you live, as I do, in a University city, you can't fail to be aware of it. Sex is one of the areas that has recently attracted the attention of the legislature. Race is another. In both these areas the law, which, as I have pointed out, in many respects distinguishes between different categories of people, taking their differences into account in the provisions it makes for them and the duties it imposes on them—in both these areas, I say, the law positively forbids discrimination. Of course, it is discrimination against one category or another, not simple discrimination between them, that is forbidden.

The Sex Discrimination Act of 1975 forbids discrimination against persons on grounds of sex in employment, education, and a number of other fields. The Race Relations Act of 1976—which is closely modelled on the Sex Discrimination Act in its definition of discrimination, and indeed, follows it word for word in several important contexts—the Race Relations Act forbids discrimination against persons on grounds of race or nationality. Sometimes, in their effort to make their point, these Acts verge upon the ridiculous. For instance, Section 25 of the Sex Discrimination Act runs as follows: 'In the Midwives Act of 1951 all references to women shall be deemed to refer to men, except references to women in childbirth'.

But the main purpose of each of the two Acts is plain. Certain differences between people must be disregarded by their fellow-citizens in large and important areas of social life. How can this novel and unheard of interference with the liberty of the individual citizen be justified? I think that the main objective of these laws is the preservation of law and order, and the prevention of conflict between different groups. That is certainly a commendable object, and justifies the law in forbidding discrimination which would be likely to lead to a breach of the peace.

Of course, decent people, good citizens, don't go about stirring up hatred among their fellow-men, setting people of one class, or one race, or one nation, against another. It is certainly wrong to do this in time of peace. In time of war, perhaps different considerations apply. We were right,

97

surely, to hate Hitler and the Nazis, and to encourage our fellow-citizens to hate them. But did it become right to do this only when war was actually declared? I am afraid that I began to hate Hitler and all he stood for, and to encourage others to do so, way back in the mid-thirties, when war was still several years off. And, when war is declared, what is the duty of the truly religious man, the truly good man, whose religion tells him that he ought to love his enemies? There is plenty of scope for casuistry and argument here. (Incidentally, I have never really understood that Gospel injunction about loving your enemies—any more than I understand what the Gospel means when it says 'love thy neighbour as thyself'. How much should we love ourselves? I had always supposed that self-love was something to be reprobated).

In time of peace, surely the law should confine its interference in these matters to preserving public order. The provisions of the Race Relations Act which forbid a shop-keeper (for instance) to refuse to supply goods to a person belonging to a certain racial group, are justified, surely, by the existence in certain parts of the country of racial tension, which might be sparked into actual violence by such discriminatory behaviour. Discrimination against certain sections of the public is not wrong in itself. The law does not forbid a shopkeeper to say that he will not supply goods to red-headed men, or men over six feet high, or Christian Scientists, or people with surnames containing more than ten letters. Such discrimination may be as foolish as it would be capricious, but there is no reason why it should be made a criminal offence. It wouldn't be likely to lead to riots on behalf of red-headed men.

What then about the Sex Discrimination Act? Why shouldn't a man open a bar for men only? Or a tea-shop for women only? Why shouldn't someone employ men (or women) only in his business, and frame his advertisements for staff vacancies accordingly? There is, surely, not such tension between the sexes in this country as would lead to an outbreak of violence if advertisements of the kind forbidden by the Act were published. But such tension in a multi-racial society, such as we have, for better or worse, become, is a real danger, and I think it is very proper that the law, at any rate until racial feelings become a thing of the past, should forbid discrimination against individuals on racial grounds. But I can see no necessity and, indeed, no justification in Britain today, for such wide-ranging provisions against sex-discrimination as are contained in the Sex Discrimination Act. In other words, I am not (I hope!) a racist or a racialist, but I'm afraid I may have earned the label 'Male Chauvinist Pig'.

Lying

I have just been reading a fascinating book on a fascinating subject. It is called *Lying*. As its name suggests, it's about telling the truth—and not telling the truth. Should we always tell the truth? Are all lies wrong? Are all untruths lies? When, if ever, is it permissible to tell a downright lie, with the intention of deceiving? Are there any circumstances in which it is not only permissible but positively *right* to tell a lie, and *wrong* to tell the truth? Of course, these questions are the stock-in-trade of moral philosophers and ethical theorists, but they are questions that also confront ordinary people—though they mayn't realize it—every day of their lives. It is questions of this kind, at the same time philosophical and practical, that are dealt with in the book *Lying*.

The author of *Lying* is Sissela Bok, the wife of Derek Bok, the President of Harvard University, and daughter of Gunnar Myrdal, the Swedish economist. Sissela Bok is a teacher in the Harvard Medical School, and her field is medical ethics. She is concerned especially with the duty of a doctor to his patients, particularly patients who are desperately ill. Should the doctor tell them, if they ask—'Doctor, I want to know the truth!'—how ill they are, when he knows that a truthful answer might diminish their chances of survival, or, if death is certain, make their last hours miserable, while an untruthful, cheerful answer might save their lives, or at least enable them to die with their minds at peace? Sissela Bok discusses those problems and kindred problems arising over the whole range of public and private life. As I've said, her study of them is fascinating: I couldn't put her book down. She *made* me *think*; and I should like to share some of my thoughts with my listeners.

Let us start in the nursery. 'Always tell the truth' you say to a child. 'Why?' 'Because it's wrong, it's *naughty*, to tell lies:' In the nursery, no doubt, that will do for an answer. But suppose we are asked 'Why is it wrong? Why is it naughty?' Well, I think there are two reasons why lying is wrong—though it might be difficult to explain them to a child. The first is what might be called a social reason, the second is a personal one.

First, the smooth running of society depends upon its members being able to trust each other: human intercourse consists largely of verbal communication; words are the currency we use in order to convey information and to exchange ideas; every time we tell a lie we—well! I won't say we debase the currency, but we put a false coin into circulation. If our lie is detected, public trust in the currency suffers. And, whether or not a particular lie is detected, the knowledge that lying is a generally accepted practice would undermine mutual confidence, with a damaging effect upon social life. We can't live easily together unless we known that we can trust one another. That is a social, practical, extrinsic reason why lying is wrong and bad. The other reason is a personal, intrinsic, almost you might say, an æsthetic reason. It is simply that nice people, the kind of people one likes and would wish one's self to be, don't habitually tell lies, or deceive; deceitfulness is an unattractive characteristic. I remember my philosophy tutor at Oxford saying 'Why don't we tell lies? *Because we don't want to become liars.*' If we overheard someone discussing our characters, what is the remark about ourselves that we should least like to hear? I sometimes ask myself that question. Well! 'A little of him goes a long way. He's an awful bore'—that would be pretty bad; but 'He's a terrible liar; one can't trust a word he says'—I think that would be a great deal worse.

Of course it may be that the reason why we regard honesty as an attractive characteristic is really a social one; what we think of as simply an æsthetic judgment may have a subconscious utilitarian basis—that is a question for sociologists and psychologists. I can only say that I should find that explanation difficult to accept. I can't believe that when we say, in praise of a friend, that he is 'a delightful character—sincere, open, honest as the day is long,' we are really praising him for his civic virtue. Truthfulness may be a civic virtue, useful to society; it is also a habit of mind, a disposition that adds attractiveness to individuals who display it. There is something likeable about open-hearted, straight-forward people; deviousness is as unattractive in a friend as it is undesirable in someone with whom we are doing business.

Another practical reason has been suggested for cultivating the habit of telling the truth; truthfulness may be best not only for society but for the truth-teller himself. Lying is a kind of dishonesty, and '*Honesty*,' the proverb tells us, '*is the best policy*:' You'll get on best in the world if people trust you because they know you always mean what you say. I have two or three comments to make on that proverb. First, I'm not sure, if that's what it means, that it is true. I don't think you can say that honesty *always* 'pays off.' Second, if it *is* true, it's a very poor reason for telling people to be honest: 'Honesty is the best policy,' said Archbishop Whately, 'but he who is governed by that maxim is not an honest man.' Calculating honesty, or calculated honesty, when one

103

comes to think of it, really is a contradiction in terms.

My third comment is that I don't think that the popular interpretation of the proverb is the correct one. Ninety-nine people out of a hundred take it to mean simply that habitual honesty 'pays off;' giving 'policy' its modern sense of 'course of action.' I don't think that's what 'Honesty is the best policy' really means: its message is a subtler and more cynical one than that. The proverb dates back to the days when 'policy' had its original meaning of craftiness and cunning: 'Honesty is the best policy' means that honesty is the best kind of cunning: the best way to deceive people is to tell them the truth. 'When in doubt,' said Mark Twain, 'tell the truth. It will confound your enemies and astound your friends.'

Well! whatever may be meant by 'Honesty is the best policy', I think everyone—and by 'everyone' I mean all sensible, decent people; I exclude fools and rogues—agrees that lying is to be condemned both on utilitarian social grounds and on moral personal grounds, both because truth-telling helps to make the world go round and because honest, truthful, people are more likeable and admirable than liars.

But should we *always* tell the truth? Aren't there occasions, situations, when it is permissible, even *right*, to deceive people by telling them what

104

isn't true? That is the question that Sissela Bok deals with in *Lying*. She surveys the whole field—politics, business, private life, the family, the lawyer and his clients, the doctor and his patients, and the schoolmaster or University teacher and the pupil for whom he is writing a testimonial—may he exaggerate his pupil's merits, when he knows that all his rivals are over-praising *their* candidates?—and she raises a host of practical problems about truth-telling and deceit in those varied contexts. She also assembles in an interesting Appendix relevant passages from nine philosophers and writers on ethics during the past 1500 years, from St Augustine and Thomas Aquinas, through Francis Bacon and Kant, down to Sir Roy Harrod and Mr G. J. Warnock, Principal of Hertford College, Oxford. (Incidentally, though I can't claim to have been personally acquainted with St Augustine or Thomas Aquinas, I am proud to have enjoyed the friendship of the two last-mentioned writers. Two out of nine is surely not bad!).

Most people, while agreeing that it is always, or almost always, wrong to tell a *lie*, would hold that there are circumstances in which an untruth doesn't amount to a lie, or at least—if it is a lie—may be called an innocent lie, and that such lies are perfectly justifiable. The two most obvious examples of this kind of untruth are 'white lies,' told on social occasions, and lies told in order to deceive the enemy in time of war.

In the course of an evening party, a fellow-guest asks you what you think of her dress, which she has just brought back from Paris. And at the end of the party your hostess says she hopes you have enjoyed the evening. In fact, you thought the dress was hideous, and the evening was for you one of excruciating boredom. If you are a civilized human being, you do not tell the truth in answer to either of these questions. On such occasions, it is lying, not truth-telling, that helps to make the world go round. It is a convention, accepted by all concerned, that in such a social context truthfulness is not required. Speech was given to man, it has been said, to enable him not only to communicate his thoughts, but also to conceal them.

This is still more obviously the case about lying in war-time in order to deceive the enemy. When war is declared, it has been said, one of the first casualties is truth. War is like a game in which both sides agree that lying is not barred: neither side can complain about being deceived. No one can say that it was wicked of the Allies to deceive the Germans concerning 'D-Day'—about where and when the invasion of the Continent was to take place. Civilization depended, not on truth-telling, but upon successful lying. A committed truth-teller would of necessity be a pacifist.

In those cases—'white lies' told on social occasions, and lies told to deceive the enemy in time of war—the justification of untruthfulness is the acceptance of a convention by all concerned. There are other cases where the justification depends upon a special relationship between the deceiver and the deceived: for example, parent and child, doctor and patient, a Cabinet Minister and the public. Everyone would agree that people in such positions have a special duty about telling the truth to the people they are responsible for. What is that duty? A duty always to tell the truth—the truth, the whole truth, and nothing but the truth? No: a duty to choose rightly when to tell the truth and how much of the truth to tell, and when to deceive those who are in their charge.

A committed truth-teller—one who believes that it is right always to tell the truth, never to conceal it, and never to deceive—is not fitted, or is to that extent unfitted, to be a parent, or a doctor, or a political leader. 'Father, I cannot tell a lie,' said the infant George Washington. Did he learn how to do it before he grew up to be President of the United States? I can't help hoping—for his sake and for his country's—that he did.

I am not being cynical when I say this—just the

reverse. I am not saying that people in responsible positions should be people we cannot trust; I'm saying just the opposite of that: they should be people we *can* trust, people we can trust to tell us as much of the truth as it is good for us to know. That, surely, is quite obviously true of parents and of doctors: children and sick people, whether the physically or the mentally sick, simply cannot 'take' the truth: it must be left to those in charge of them to decide how much of the truth it is good for them to know. And it is obviously true of what are now called the 'underdeveloped' countries, where the mass of the people are not fitted, by birth or education, to take part in the government. It is not so obvious in an educated democracy. There, the rulers represent the people, and are in perpetual contact with them. They are subject to continual cross-examination by their opponents and by their own supporters in Parliament, by the electors in their constituencies, and by journalists and political commentators in the press and on the air. They have a difficult and complex rôle to play—devising party policy, drafting controversial legislation, and conducting international negotiations. They must take, or seem to take, the public into their confidence, but they have to practise an economy of truth: they can't tell all the people all the truth all the time. Up to a point, and on occasion, they must mislead them, or allow them to be misled—and this from the highest motives, and in the interests of the very people they are deceiving. Their opponents will always be vigilant to catch them out and to put the least favourable construction on their motives—and if their cover-up, however well-intentioned, is exposed, they can expect, as President Nixon discovered to his cost, no mercy from their enemies—enemies who may, incidentally, be no less devious than they are themselves.

Forget now about special occasions, where conventions permitting deception are accepted by all concerned; forget the responsibilities of people in special positions, parents, doctors, Cabinet Ministers. What about ordinary people, in the sort of situations we find ourselves in every day, when a choice is before us, to tell the truth or to tell a lie?

Take a case suggested by Dr Johnson: you are alone in the street when a man dashes past you, obviously in terror, calling out 'Help! help! save me!', and disappears down a by-street. A moment later another man rushes up to you, brandishing a pistol, and asks 'Which way did he go?' What are you to say? The committed truth-teller has no doubt about the answer. St Augustine, the Christian saint, and Immanuel Kant, the moral philosopher, agree that you should tell him the truth: you mustn't *ever* tell a lie. Others, who jib at telling the truth in such a situation, but won't admit a positive lie in any circumstances, say: 'Don't tell him anything—just knock him down!' 'But if he's twice my size?' 'Then pretend you don't know which way his victim went.' 'But if he puts his pistol to my head and says "You saw which way he went: tell me!" Must I still either tell him the truth or say nothing and get killed?' My own answer would be 'No! tell him a lie'—but then, I'm not a Christian saint or a moral philosopher.

Of course, you can invent dozens of cases that pose this problem—indeed, you don't have to invent them, they arise every day, between members of a family, professional men and their clients, business associates, business rivals—a whole range of such cases is dealt with in Sissela Bok's treatise. The way you answer them, I think, depends upon the kind of person you are—whether you are someone who is consciously guided by *a priori* principles—'always do this', 'never do that'—or an empiricist, who acts partly by instinct, partly from a calculation of the results of his actions. For the committed truth-teller no difficulty arises in such cases: 'Always tell the truth.' The casuist and the philosopher may interpose a difficult question here: 'What is the truth? And need you tell the *whole* truth? And can anyone ever know—let alone, *tell*—the whole

110

truth about anything?' But apart from such philosophical difficulties, the difference between the reaction of the committed truth-teller and that of the ordinary man is absolute—there is for him no question of envisaging the consequences, of calculating the benefit and the harm that will accrue to either side, and to society as a whole, if he departs from the rule. The ordinary man, on the other hand, will be guided partly by calculation, but still more by instinct. He will take into account the likelihood, so far as he is able to estimate it, that his lie will be detected, and the harm that will be done to society, if it is detected, by his having put this particular false coin into circulation; and on the other side of the balance he will place the benefit that will accrue to individuals, himself or others, or the harm they will be saved from, if his deception is successful.

Of course, I am not suggesting that lying for personal gain or for other selfish—or even altruistic—motives is justified whenever it can be carried through without detection. You may only do evil—and lying is *prima facie* an evil—that *good* may come. How much good, and what kind of good, justifies a lie, that is the question, and it is a question on which I do not profess to lay down any rule. Instinct is the best guide: plainly one should not do anything of which one would be instinctively ashamed: lying for personal profit is obviously such a thing. But the doctor's lie to the patient who is mortally ill, an unselfish lie told in order to mitigate the sufferings of another—is that a thing that he should be ashamed of, and if he need not be ashamed of the lie, does that not justify his telling it? I do not offer any answer, or any rule or guide for others for the answering of such questions. It is the merit of Sissela Bok's treatment of the field of lying that she makes you think about these problems, not that she provides solutions for them.

No rules, no principles: the world comes to us ready-made, and we must deal with it as best we can, facing our difficulties with a clear head, well screwed on, and a warm heart in the right place.

Perhaps some lines I found in an old commonplace book may not be irrelevant here:

> Two Lords there are to whose commands I bow:
> The Rough and Ready, and the Here and Now.
> On three resources rests my confidence:
> A seemly cloak of civilized pretence,
> And common decency, and common sense.

Not a very idealistic way of looking at the world, you may say; but, if we live up to it, I don't think we need be ashamed of any departure from the truth that it entails.

Let me conclude with an anecdote about a well-known Oxford figure of the Victorian age, Benjamin Jowett, the Master of Balliol College.

Jowett, like all Heads of Colleges in those days, was in Holy Orders. He was a Broad Churchman—so broad that some doubt was cast upon his orthodoxy; but no one doubted that he was a Christian and an honest man.

The story goes that an Oxford tradesman was sorely worried by the strain put upon his conscience by the conditions of business competition, and he decided to seek the advice of the Master of Balliol. He was granted an interview by Jowett, and laid his perplexities before the Master. He explained that he was a faithful member of the Church of England and (he hoped) a good Christian: he did his best, in all the ups and downs of life, to follow out the precepts of the Gospels, and in particular to be honest and to tell the truth. He had a wife and children to support, and he maintained them by carrying on the family business. Competition was keen and—it was here that his difficulty arose—his business rivals were unscrupulous. They cheated shamelessly and without restraint. It was impossible to carry on his business successfully unless—to put it plainly—he cheated too, and outcheated his competitors. What was he to do? Cheating was repugnant to him. But if he carried on his business at a loss, or if he had to wind it up, he was ruined, and his family would starve. What advice had the Master to give him?

Jowett listened to his story patiently, and did not interrupt him. Then he gave his considered advice. It was contained in six short words: 'Cheat as little as you can.'

What would Sissela Bok have to say to this? I am not quite sure. It is one of the great merits of her book that she lays down no rigid rules: she is very realistic and full of practical common sense. In her concluding chapter—which contains an excellent summary of the whole question—she has some wise words about business codes of ethics and the deceptive practices they are supposed to eliminate but which they sometimes (as in the scandal about General Electric in 1960) conceal and actually protect. Such practices, she concludes, 'in an imperfect world cannot be wiped out altogether, but surely they can be reduced.'

That is not far off what Jowett said to the Oxford tradesman. But there is a touch of cynicism in the way Jowett put it which Mrs Bok would, I think, find distasteful, and his verdict would certainly have shocked St Augustine and St Thomas Aquinas and Immanuel Kant. But it would, I am sure, have had Dr Johnson's approval, and I think that it has mine also.

Reflections on Punishment

This talk has for its title 'Reflections on Punishment.' A better title for it might have been 'Some questions about punishment'; for what I have to say will really consist of a series of questions— questions to which I can't myself, in most cases, offer a decided answer. The first of these questions is 'What does the word "punishment" mean?'.

Like most words, of course, it has several meanings, or, rather, its meaning varies in accordance with the context in which we use it.

Our earliest notions of punishment—at any rate, if we had an old-fashioned education—probably came from the Bible; the word has theological associations: 'punishment for sin', 'Divine retribution', 'eternal punishment'. Dr Johnson, you may remember, confessed to a friend that he was afraid that he would be damned; and when his friend asked him what he meant by 'damned', replied 'Sent to Hell, Sir, and punished everlastingly'.

Well! I'm not concerned with theology, with the punishment inflicted by divine agency upon human beings; the kind of punishment I want to discuss is the punishment that's inflicted, or imposed, by some human beings upon others—in the nursery by parents, or in schools by teachers, or in the adult world by what is called 'the machinery of justice.'

Of course, punishment, in whatever sphere it occurs, means that the victim, the person who undergoes it, is in some way (to use an unpleasant but convenient neologism) 'disadvantaged'—he suffers 'in purse or person', as the old legal textbooks put it. It also implies that he has brought the suffering upon himself: he is paying the penalty for something he has done.

But I don't think that, in ordinary speech or thought, we regard all penalties imposed by the law as punishments. In the old railway carriages there used to be a cord—there still is, I think, in some of them—called the 'communication cord,' which bore a notice 'In case of emergency, pull cord', with the added warning 'Penalty for improper use £5'. Well! If you pulled the cord, as young persons sometimes did, just for the pleasure of bringing the train to a halt, you were fined £5. Was that a punishment? Or was it just a penalty, a fine payable for a breach of the regulations?

Let me take another example of a penalty that seems to me—shall I say?—marginally a punish-

116

ment. The other day, I was stopped in my car by a policeman, who pointed out that I was doing over 30 miles an hour—it wasn't all that much over 30—inside—it was only *just* inside—the 30 miles an hour limit area. I duly received a summons, pleaded guilty, and had to pay a fine. I must say, I didn't regard that fine as a punishment; I regarded it simply as a penalty, the price I had to pay for breaking the law—and (I may add) breaking it unwittingly, for I didn't realize that I was doing more than 30 miles an hour. Does the fact that I didn't realize that I was exceeding the speed limit affect the answer to the question whether the fine I paid was just a penalty, or a punishment also? I think it does.

Surely punishment implies some sort of moral guilt on the part of the individual who has incurred it. Of course, a conscious and intentional breach of the law is in itself, *prima facie*, an immoral act. When we deliberately break (or 'flout') the law, we put ourselves above, or outside, the law; and by so doing we set a bad example to our fellow-citizens, and to that extent reduce the general public respect for the law and confidence in it. A deliberate breach of the law is, of itself, an immoral act.

There may be more or less fully extenuating circumstances which reduce the moral guilt to zero, or practically zero, even if the act was intentional.

117

If the act was not intentional, or if fully extenuating circumstances exist, then, though the breach of the law remains, there is no moral guilt, and the fine exacted by the law should be considered, I suggest, to be not a punishment, but simply a penalty.

Punishment, then, is the infliction of pain or suffering upon an individual because he has done something morally wrong.

It may be imposed either by the State, as a penalty for a breach of the law of the land, or by a private person in a position of authority—a parent in the nursery, for instance, or a teacher in a school.

Certainly, the imposition of punishment implies a duly instituted, or recognized, authority. When a brute or a bully exclaims 'I'll *punish* you for this!' he is, no doubt unconsciously, assuming authority; he is using a metaphor borrowed from the field of morals; if he chose his words carefully—which brutes and bullies don't usually bother to do—he'd say 'I'll make you suffer for this!' or 'I'll make you pay for this!' In every-day life, we often use the same moral metaphor about the sufferings we bring upon ourselves simply by our own foolishness or carelessness: 'I didn't put on a mackintosh, and I was punished for it by catching a terrible cold', or 'I was punished for dawdling over tea: I missed the 4·45!' What we

118

ought to say, of course, is simply 'I paid the penalty'; but the influence of ethics upon our vocabulary is too strong, and the moral metaphor creeps in.

It was, I think, because punishment implies the assumption of moral authority by the State that it had a bad name with the Utilitarians. 'All punishment is mischief' said Jeremy Bentham; 'all punishment in itself is evil'. As a matter of fact, I think he went further than that: punishment involved pain or suffering; all pain is evil, therefore punishment *per se* is evil.

What he meant, I suggest, was: 'There should be no punishment; only penalties. Penalties are for law-breaking. Punishment is for sin. And sin, if there is such a thing, is no concern of the State.' Do we agree with that? The State has the power of making laws and inflicting penalties; how far, if at all, should it use its legislative power in order to uphold moral standards and enforce moral behaviour—or, at least, prevent immoral behaviour?

There are large areas in which no one would challenge the State's right to legislate, and where no question of morality arises—where there would be no duty to do what the law requires us to do if the law didn't require it, and no duty to refrain from doing what the law forbids us to do if the law didn't forbid it.

Examples that spring to mind are the areas

119

covered by the Finance Acts, imposing taxation, by the Road Traffic Acts (speed regulations, safety precautions, insurance requirements), by the Licensing Acts (governing the purchase and sale of liquor), and by the Acts that control the erection and construction of buildings (ensuring that they conform to 'health requirements', or that they don't spoil the countryside).

Then there is an area—and it is the area that most criminal legislation is concerned with—in which the conduct forbidden by law is also an offence against accepted morality—notably, offences against property or the person, like theft, obtaining money by false pretences, assault, rape, murder. Benthamite utilitarians would agree with moralistic political philosophers on the propriety of the State's legislating against such conduct, though Benthamites might disagree with other political philosophers about how severely, in particular cases, such offences should be punished: the measure of the punishment, they would say, should be governed by its effectiveness as an instrument of reforming the prisoner and preventing others from imitating him, regardless of the moral turpitude involved in his offence.

Finally, there is the disputed area, in which the law intervenes simply and solely in the interests of morality. The cases arising in this area are a very mixed bag, and there is plenty of scope for disagreement about them. Personally, I find it impossible to take a 'line' when I'm surveying this area: I don't think naturally in categories, and I'm not guided—consciously at any rate—by principles; I am much more liable to be swayed by intuition, and intuition is not a consistent mentor.

Take a few examples of conduct forbidden by the law simply (or so it seems to me) on moral grounds. (I am assuming throughout—and you must always bear this in mind—that the conduct in question does not take place in circumstances likely to outrage public decency or to create disorder).

First, Female Prostitution: it is not a criminal offence for a woman to sell her body (I use the crude old phrase). But it is a criminal offence for a man to 'live on the immoral earnings of a woman.' Why? I have never done so myself, and am unlikely, I think, ever to be tempted to do so; but, if I did, why should I be deemed to be guilty of a criminal offence?

Then, take blackmail. Odious behaviour, no doubt; abominable, detestable—the sort of conduct that no decent person would indulge in. But I confess that, though I am in no hurry to have the law forbidding it removed from the Statute-book, I don't see why blackmail should be a criminal offence.

And what about cruelty? Here I can speak with

perfect detachment, but not (I am afraid) with perfect consistency. I can speak with detachment because, though I was born with a temperament that leaves me a prey to many temptations, the temptation to be cruel, to animals or to human beings, is not one of them—it just doesn't come naturally to me. (I dare say it's due to laziness or lack of imagination on my part—but there it is!) But why should the law intervene to prevent cruelty to animals, provided it does not take place in public, and the victim is the property of the person charged with the offence?

Cruelty to children, yes: I may be inconsistent, but I can't help approving of the series of Acts, culminating in the Children and Young Persons Act, 1933, passed in order to prevent cruelty to children. To justify that legislation, it isn't necessary to hold that it is a function of the law to enforce moral principles. If the State is interested in preventing cruelty, on moral grounds, why should it limit its interference to cases where the victim is a child? No: it isn't *cruelty*, it is *suffering*, that the State is interested in preventing, and it intervenes on behalf of those—children and animals—who are unable to protect themselves.

(That, perhaps, goes for blackmail also: the purpose of the law, it may be said, is to protect the blackmailer's victim, not to punish the blackmailer for being wicked).

122

Perhaps I have dwelt too long on the issues raised by upholders of the doctrine that the State should not interfere in the field of private morality. For today it is the voice not of the utilitarian, but of the humanitarian, that is loudest in this field. The topic that today seems most to engage the minds of the thinkers and critics concerned is not the range and scope of the criminal law, but the problem of how to treat the convicted criminal: punishment, not crime; penology rather than criminology.

It is a complex, fascinating, important, and insoluble problem—and, as I said, all I can do is to pose a few questions and offer a few reflections on it—the reflections not of an expert, but of an outsider. True, I practised myself for many years at the Bar, but my field as a Chancery barrister was far removed from the Criminal law: so far as the Criminal law is concerned I am (to use the old judicial phrase) the man on the Clapham omnibus, or (as I suppose one should say nowadays) the man in the Piccadilly Tube.

The topics that crop up most frequently in popular discussions of penology are capital and corporal punishment under the criminal law and corporal punishment in schools.

The problems presented by capital and corporal punishment, however, difficult and important as they are, are, after all, relevant in only a very small

123

minority of cases. I discuss these problems at some length in my lecture on *Humanity*, printed later in this collection, see pp. 194–230 below. How is the State to punish the run-of-the-mill offender? That is the real problem. Make the punishment fit the crime? Easier said than done —except perhaps in the small self-contained childish world of the nursery; it can hardly be operated by Judges, who have to deal, in accordance with the provisions of the Statute-book, with a mixed bag of professional crooks, bandits and confidence tricksters, as well as ordinary citizens who have, in one way or another, fallen foul of the criminal law.

There is, it is true, one crime for which there is a perfectly appropriate penalty or punishment: if a man is convicted of repeated motoring offences, *deprive him of his driving licence*. But if, after that, he is caught driving without a licence—what do you do to him then? You are back where you started.

For certain offences, the law provides a scale of fines—and fining surely is a desirable alternative, where appropriate, to sending a man to prison. But if the convicted criminal is wealthy, he may be able to pay easily, while, if he's poor, he may not be able to pay at all. There doesn't seem to be much justice there!

There remains the obvious alternative: lock him up in a not too comfortable building, where he will live, for a stated number of months or years, cut off from his home and from the outside world, with a number of other convicted criminals. Prison! That is a subject that could occupy me for another twenty minutes, or more.

Prison reform: is there anyone who isn't in favour of it? Is there anyone who thinks that our prison system is perfect? (I'm not talking about the administration of the system, but about the system itself). There is no area of public debate in which there is more widespread agreement about the need for reforms, or a greater variety of conflicting views about what those reforms should be. People aren't agreed, to begin with, about what is the primary purpose of imprisonment, let alone about how to give effect to any of its purposes. And even if agreement were reached, the practical difficulties of carrying out any proposed reform are, to put it mildly, formidable—over-crowding of inmates, impossibility of recruiting adequate prison staff, and the exorbitant cost to the State of building, and of running, new and efficient prisons. Prison conditions should not be intolerably grim, on the one hand; they should not be *too* comfortable, on the other— we all know that. But where and how do we draw the line? We don't draw it—or, at any rate, it is a wavering one. 'The best that we can do' might fairly be inscribed on the gates of our penitentiary establishments. Not a very proud boast—but better, at any rate, than 'Abandon hope, all ye who enter here!'

Let's Get Rid Of . . .

I must confess that when I was given the opportunity of contributing to this series of talks I was greatly tempted to discuss a possible reform of the law that I have been advocating for many years (not publicly, but in private, among my friends)—a reform that I would bring in without delay if I became dictator. It relates to the issue of dog-licences. The object of the reform would be to restrict severely the private ownership of dogs. Police-dogs would, of course, be permitted; but licences for privately owned dogs would be granted only in respect of dogs for blind or otherwise disabled persons; guard dogs kept for the protection of their owner or his property; foxhounds and other dogs kept for sporting purposes; greyhounds kept for the purpose of racing.

This would be a far-reaching and, in my opinion, an extremely beneficial reform of the law. As I say, if I were dictator, I would introduce it without delay. But since I see no chance of my becoming dictator, and no chance of getting the reform .adopted unless I do become dictator, I won't attempt to make a case for it now by expatiating upon the beneficial effects that it would have.

Let me add a word for the reassurance of dog-lovers—I can almost hear their indignant protests ringing in my ears. *Don't take me too seriously*! It is true—I won't attempt to disguise the fact—that I am not a dog-lover myself; I am just the opposite of a dog-lover: I dislike dogs, and it's their *dogginess*—their *caninity*, if there is such a word—that puts me off them. But I can make exceptions: there have been individual dogs that I have tolerated, and been on friendly terms with, dogs that I have even been fond of. And I would gladly insert into my proposed law a provision for the grant of dog-licences, in addition to the exceptional cases I've already mentioned, to persons approved, after a due hearing (and, perhaps, after inspection of the dog for which the licence was being asked), by a special tribunal. But it would be difficult to specify the grounds on which such exceptional grants should be made, and I think it would be better—and fairer to the canine race in general—to ban privately owned dogs altogether (apart from the exceptions I have specified). However, since—short of dictatorial powers—there is plainly no chance of bringing this reform of the law into operation, I will say no more about it.

Instead, let me put forward a more serious suggestion which I hope may excite a fair volume of sympathy and support. I am sure that many, many people—I would almost dare to say 'most people'—who use the roads in this country, whether as pedestrians or as car-drivers, must share my feeling about *motor-cyclists*. The motor-bicycle, or motor-cycle, or motor-bike—for today both the name and the machine have been speeded up—is surely becoming a public menace—and an increasingly serious one.

I don't know the statistics: I don't know how many people in this country own motor-cycles, or how many motor-cycles are actually in use on the roads. My impression is that these numbers have increased very greatly during the last ten years or so; anyhow, motor-cyclists now present (as I said a moment ago) a real menace to other road-users. And 'road-users' means you and me—it means everyone.

Of course we all of us have a good deal to put up with as we go about the streets. Motor-cars are a nuisance to pedestrians; pedestrians are a nuisance to motorists; we'd all of us rather have the streets to ourselves—no cars when we're on foot, no blundering pedestrians when we're at the wheel.

But pedestrians and motorists are—if I may so put it—facts of life: everyone walks, everyone nowadays—men and women alike, and men and women of all ages—drives a car (or rides in a car

129

driven by someone else). You can't abolish cars in the world today, any more than you can abolish people; people and cars, for better or worse, must be accepted; pedestrians and motorists must learn to give and take, they must learn to put up with one another.

And so, I think, they do. But the motor-cycle is a special case. It's a luxury enjoyed by a very small section of the population. You have only to use your eyes to see that the riders of motor-bikes belong to a narrowly limited class. Very, very few of them are females—old or young. And very few of them are old, or even elderly, men. You don't see old ladies or old gentlemen whizzing along the roads, at breakneck speeds, on their motor-bikes. Almost all motor-cyclists, unless my eyes deceive me, are young men. And why are they riding motor-bikes?

Are they on some urgent business errand? Of course the motor-cycle is a necessity for army dispatch-riders, for police officers, for hospital staff who have to deal with urgent cases. But 99 out of 100 of the young men one sees on motor-cycles quite plainly don't belong to any of these categories: they are evidently, most of them, just young men out to enjoy themselves on a motor-bike. And what does their enjoyment consist in? In going as fast as possible, however much traffic there is to compete against, and however much inconvenience they may cause to their fellow-citizens. Pedal cyclists are comparatively innocent, they travel quietly and at a moderate speed; but the motor-bikes! First, they're terribly noisy, and their owners seem to be, many of them, proud of the noise they make; second, they're capable of going exceedingly fast, and their owners (as I said) seem to enjoy going as fast as possible; third, they are very heavy objects, and that, combined with the speed at which they are driven, makes them a danger to other traffic. The law seems to recognise the special danger attaching to the motor-cycle, by requiring motor-cyclists to wear crash-helmets, in case of accident.

If an accident does happen, the helmet protects its wearer—but not anyone else who may be involved in the accident. Indeed, knowledge of his own security must tempt the motor-cyclist into taking risks he wouldn't otherwise have taken. Motor-cyclists, or most of them, are not, I should say, unskilful drivers—quite the reverse. It is their skill, and their desire to show it off, or to put it to the test, that makes them such a menace to their fellow-motorists. One sees them weaving in and out of the traffic, passing now on the right side, now on the wrong, and taking off at traffic lights before the red has changed to green. They've developed a habit, too, which other motorists nowadays seem to be imitating, of switching on

131

their head-lamps in broad daylight. Why do they do it? I can only assume it means 'Look out! I'm coming: be prepared for anything!'

Well! What, you may ask, do you propose to do about it? All I can do is to lean out of the driver's window and shake my fist at the worst offenders as they pass by—and I've given up doing even that since I read about the driver who put his arm out of the window to remonstrate with a motor-cyclist who was halted alongside him at some traffic lights. The motor-cyclist took hold of his arm, broke it, and was off and away as the light turned from red to green.

What can the law do? Short of an accident, how can you catch the motor-cyclist, and prove an offence against him? And what sort of punishment would be both just and effective? No: prevention is better than cure, better than punishment. I would suggest a law limiting the grant of motor-cycle licences (except to members of the police force, the Army, hospital staffs and the like) to persons over 60 years of age. And whether or not that reform is approved, I would strongly urge that the wearing of crash-helmets should be forbidden.

But I'm afraid I'd have to be a dictator to get that law through: the votes of the manufacturers, and the importers, of motor-bicycles, and the votes of all the eighteen-year-olds, would be against me.

So please don't take this suggestion any more seriously than you took (or I hope you took) my suggestion about dog-licences!

The Sin of Pride

Study to show thyself approved unto God, a workman that needeth not to be ashamed, rightly dividing the word of truth.

2 TIMOTHY ii 15

I should not embark upon my discourse to-day without a word of gratitude to Mr William Master, whose munificence instituted more than two centuries ago this annual sermon on the Sin of Pride, and to the Vice-Chancellor, who invited me this year to deliver it. To a member of the University who is not in Holy Orders, an invitation to occupy this pulpit certainly presents a challenge; but it also confers upon him an honour, and I am proud to have been selected for the task.

'Proud'! I had better be careful what I say: have I unguardedly confessed to being guilty of a deadly sin?

Pride, like charity, covers (though in a different sense of the word 'covers') a multitude of sins, and a multitude also of attributes or dispositions or feelings that are not, I think, sins at all. Let me try to analyse, treading if I can a middle path between the shallows of verbal pedantry on the one hand and the deeps of theological speculation on the other, the various uses to which the word is put, the various things we mean by it.

First, in every-day speech we often use the word 'pride' or 'proud' in a sense which, if we are sincere, implies no presumption on our part: 'I am proud to have met you'; 'I am proud to have been invited'; we may surely use the word thus (as I used it myself a moment or two ago) without confessing to anything like a sin. All that we mean, in such cases, is that we are delighted at some favour, or some stroke of good fortune, which does not imply any merit on our part, so that really to use the word 'proud' in such a context is inappropriate. Perhaps this was that inspired the rebuke administered by the Duke of Wellington to the stranger who had the good fortune to help him across the road outside Apsley House, and when taking his leave, said that that chance meeting had made that day the proudest day of his life. The Duke's rejoinder, couched in terms not suitable to be repeated in this pulpit, really meant, I think, that, while to have met a great man might be a stroke of good fortune, it was nothing really to be proud of. Indeed, on such occasions it is our modesty, if we are sincere, that makes us say that we are proud.

Akin to this modest pride is what may be called 'vicarious pride': the satisfaction we may feel in

135

belonging to a body or institution that is worthy of respect. Many of us—or, at least, many of the older among us—must have been exhorted in our childhood and in our youth to take a pride in our school, in our regiment, in our country. What was the meaning and purpose of such exhortations? Here again I think that the feeling our masters, or our mentors, were referring to was not really pride in the strict sense. What they meant was 'You are lucky enough—for it is due to no merit of your own—to belong to a body of persons worthy of respect: don't be ashamed of them; don't let them down; do them credit. You owe it to them to behave in a manner that is worthy of them. Make plain to the world the pleasure that it gives you to be one of their number.'

If that is pride, it is surely not a sinful pride; it is a virtue rather than a vice. I call it 'vicarious pride', not 'proper pride', because in such cases our membership of the body we are proud of is due to no merit of our own.

What then is 'proper pride'? It is, I think the satisfaction we evince—that is, that we both feel and show—in something for which we are ourselves responsible. Pride in our work, for instance, pride in our achievements, pride in our appearance, pride in ourselves. These, again, were feelings instilled into us or encouraged by the mentors of our youth. What they were saying to us when they told us to take a pride in our work, say, or in our appearance, was surely this: 'You are the possessor of certain gifts and certain qualities, you have produced work that is in itself a proof of these: don't under-value your gifts, whether intellectual or physical; make the most of your natural excellences; don't be ashamed of them; be ashamed, rather, of work that is not as good as you can make it; to be content with anything less than your best is unworthy of you as a human being.' This was a perfectly legitimate appeal to proper pride. For if we should be ashamed of our failures, of scamped or second-rate work, it is a natural, if not a necessary, corollary that we should be pleased with—and (yes!) proud of—our successes, of work that is as good as we can make it. That is a proper pride, whether it relates to our products, to our achievements, or indeed to our appearance.

> Yes, I am proud: I must be proud, to see
> Men not afraid of God, afraid of me.

Those lines of Pope, expressing satisfaction in the effectiveness of his satire, were an effusion of proper pride. He was using, surely, the language of Aristotle's Μεγαλόψυχος ἄνηρ—called 'the proud man' by Aristotle's Oxford translator—the man who 'thinks himself worthy of great things, being worthy of them,' and 'claims honour in accordance with his deserts.'

So far, so good; and by 'good' I mean *good*: the pride I have been describing, proper pride, is a virtue, not a vice. What now of improper pride, the pride that oversteps the boundary between good and evil, or is born (so to speak) on the wrong side of it? Well! improper pride may be of several different kinds—there are several diseases to which proper pride, or the possessor of proper pride, is liable. Self-respect may swell into self-satisfaction; self-satisfaction, in persons of a certain temperament, may take the odious form of smugness; one's good opinion of one's self, even if justifiable and adequately founded, may blossom into conceit. One may be too pleased, or too obviously pleased, with one's self; one may 'give one's self airs'. All these failings have to do with a person's good opinion of himself, and the effect that that opinion has upon his behaviour—an effect that will vary in accordance with his character or temperament.

There is one failing, somewhat akin to those I have been trying to describe, which must yet be distinguished from them: I mean, vanity. About that, I must say a special word. Vanity is something quite distinct from pride. I will not say that vanity and pride cannot both be present in the same character, but I think it is true to say that the prouder a man is, the less room there is in him for vanity. The prouder a man is, the less he cares what others think about him. It was with this in mind that Swift said shrewdly of one of his contemporaries that he was 'too proud to be vain'.

It is easiest, perhaps, to appreciate the difference between the proud man and the vain man by considering actual examples, in fiction or in real life. One does not have to look very far in any society—least of all in an academic society, which affords a rich soil for vanity and pride—to come upon excellent specimens of either character. I have in mind in particular two old friends, old friends of mine and, I don't doubt old friends of many in this congregation, who seem to me to display all too clearly the attributes of vanity, in the one case, and pride, in the other. I mean Sir Walter Elliot, of Kellynch Hall in the county of Somerset, and Sir Leicester Dedlock, of Chesney Wold in the county of Lincoln.

Of Sir Walter Elliot his creator says 'Vanity was the beginning and the end of Sir Walter Elliot's character; vanity of person and of situation. He had been remarkably handsome in his youth; and, at fifty-four, was still a very fine man. Few women could think more of their personal appearance than he did. . . . He considered the blessing of beauty as inferior only to the blessing of a baronetcy; and the Sir Walter Elliot, who united these gifts, was the constant object of his warmest respect and devotion'. Sir Walter found little to admire, Jane Austen tells us, in the looks of his daughter Anne, 'so totally different were her delicate features and mild dark eyes from his own'.

Sir Walter Elliot was a vain man: he cared about the figure he cut, about how he appeared to other people. Sir Leicester Dedlock was made of sterner stuff: he 'is only a baronet', says Dickens, 'but there is no mightier baronet than he. His family is as old as the hills, and infinitely more respectable. He has a general opinion that the world might get on without hills, but would be done up without Dedlocks. . . . He is a gentleman of strict conscience, disdainful of all littleness and meanness. . . He is an honourable, obstinate, truthful, high-spirited, intensely prejudiced, perfectly unreasonable man. . . . He supposes all his dependants to be utterly bereft of individual characters, intentions, or opinions, and is persuaded that he was born to supersede the necessity of their having any'.

Sir Leicester was a proud man, and his pride was bad, not good. Did it amount to a deadly sin? For the subject of this sermon, I should remind you, is the *Sin* of Pride, and Pride is one of the Seven Deadly Sins—indeed, the Fathers of the Church, and the scholastic writers who classified the Seven Deadly Sins, put *Superbia* first—gave it (should I say?) pride of place—among them.

We should reflect for a moment not merely on what we mean by pride, but on what we mean by sin, and more particularly on what we mean by a deadly sin, and by punishment for sin. We shall be punished, the Scriptures tell us, for our sins, and for some sins, mortal or deadly sins, if we do not repent of them in time, we shall be punished eternally. Are we punished for what we do, or for what we are, for our sinful acts, or for our vicious dispositions? And are we punished for things we cannot help? While our actions are, most of them, within our control, our nature is something we are born with, and which, beyond a certain point, we cannot change. And our actions are very largely determined by our nature.

Such questions must present themselves to anyone who thinks, even for a little, about the sin of pride, and it would be wrong to attempt a sermon on the subject without a hint of the depth and difficulty of the problems latent in the concept of a deadly sin.

I leave these problems to the theologians, and return to the simpler question: what kind of pride is it that ranks as a deadly sin?

Pride, without any precise specification of its nature, is often held up to disapproval both in the Old Testament and in the New: 'The Lord hateth a proud look', said King Solomon, and again 'A proud heart is an abomination'. The Virgin Mary may have had such admonitions in mind when in the Magnificat she declared that the Lord had scattered the proud in the imagination of their hearts. Her Son invariably commended meekness and gentleness, and himself—though he could be roused to righteous indignation—set an example of those qualities: 'I am meek', he reminded his disciples, 'and lowly'; and he reassured the meek in his Sermon on the Mount by telling them that they would inherit the earth. Our Lord, when he said this, was not commending meekness as being itself a virtue, any more than he was commending poverty or mourning when he said that the poor and the mourners were blessed; he was comforting them. 'Be patient', he was saying to the meek, 'you will come into your own, and then you need be meek no longer'—just as, in his own good time, he himself, once meek and lowly, would come in glory to judge the quick and the dead. There is nothing in his words to the meek, or in his own profession of meekness, that is inconsistent with a due appreciation of proper pride.

What then did Our Lord think about pride? This appears most clearly, I think, from his parable about the Pharisee and the publican, which was directed, according to St. Luke, against those who 'trusted in themselves that they were righteous, and despised others'. '*And despised others'*—there is the sting of the reproof. The Pharisee took what might have been a proper pride in his own virtuous living, his honesty, his kindness, his charitable donations; there was nothing wrong, I think, in his expression of gratitude to God for endowing him with qualities superior to those of most other men. But he gave himself away by adding the words 'or even as this publican'—and (I suspect) by the tone of voice in which he uttered them. He was too ready to assume that humbler men were inferior to himself, and to despise them for that supposed inferiority.

It is the pride that is arrogance, overweening pride, over-bearing behaviour, a constitutional contempt for one's fellow men—whether in one's everyday dealings with them or in the realm of the intellect or of the spirit—that wins for pride, personal or intellectual or spiritual pride, its place among the Seven Deadly Sins.

A sermon has been preached in this church on this subject, year by year, for nearly three centuries. A historian of manners, or of morals, could tell us, no doubt, at which periods during that stretch of time admonitions against pride were called for most urgently: for particular vices wax and wane as conditions change in the society that produces them. The sin of pride was commoner, I imagine, two hundred years ago than it is today;

143

commoner still, perhaps, in those dark ages when it won its primacy among the Deadly Sins. It flourished when society was politically, socially, and economically, more definitely stratified than it is today—in an age of kings and nobles, tyrannies and aristocracies:

> Pride in their port, defiance in their eye,
> I see the Lords of human kind pass by.

The Lords of human kind hardly exist today; baronetcies of ancient lineage count for nothing, and such of them as survive are not accorded the homage that engenders and fosters arrogance and pride. Today Sir Leicester Dedlock probably travels down from London second-class, and when he arrives at Chesney Wold there are no dependants waiting on the platform to touch their caps to him—and I dare say the change is a salutary one for all concerned.

The structure of contemporary society hardly permits the existence of a class of overlords: a democracy provides no framework to sustain an aristocratic *élite*, a breeding-ground for arrogant pride. But there exists today another more important factor telling against pride: society is permeated by a strong egalitarian feeling, which refuses to acknowledge not merely *élites* of power, but any *élites* whatever, and, while consciously hostile to the pride that is a vice, is unconsciously

144

hostile even to virtuous and proper pride. Two currents in this tide make themselves felt: envy—itself a Deadly Sin—of those who are better off than one's self, and a feeling very different from envy: reluctance to admit that anybody, one's self included, is really superior to anybody else. This second current of feeling seems to me to be a feverish disease or corruption of the Grace of Humility (which is itself the subject of the companion sermon preached each year under Mr Master's benefaction). The strength of this sentiment, particularly among the younger generation, is a new and remarkable phenomenon, and it certainly deserves a sermon to itself. For it is the sworn enemy not only of the sin of pride, but also of that proper pride the virtues of which I have tried to expound today. Proper pride is, after all, the expression of a feeling of superiority, and superiority has no place in a world where all are equal: that all human beings are equal, or that we should pretend that they all are equal, is the gospel professed by many of the young, and inculcated by many of their teachers. 'Take a pride in your achievements!'—these injunctions are not often, I fancy, heard today in the schoolroom—and still less frequent, to judge by results, must be the injunction 'Take a pride in your appearance!'.

If this tide of feeling were to flood the world, the meek would indeed inherit the earth—but in a sense not, I think, intended by the author of the Beatitudes.

If a benefactor came forward today wishing to found two annual sermons to be delivered here during the next two centuries, and asked for a pair of subjects fitted for the times, he might be well advised to choose, for one, the vice of excessive humility, and for the other, the virtue of proper pride.

Marcuse and
the Gospel of Hate

Herbert Marcuse is an elderly Professor of Political Thought at San Diego in California who hates American society as it is organized today and believes that the time is at hand when an entirely new kind of community can be substituted for it. He would like to overthrow the governmental institutions and industrial machinery of the United States, to destroy the whole apparatus of the existing acquisitive and 'exploitative' society, and to liquidate the authorities who control that apparatus. Marcuse's chosen agents in effectuating this purpose, the shock troops of the social revolution, are young 'militants', most of them coloured people and students, and it is to them that he formally dedicates *An Essay on Liberation* (Allen Lane The Penguin Press, 25s), four short chapters in which he sets out the essentials of his creed.

Certainly there is much to criticise in the mechanised and materialistic America of today: its extremes of wealth and poverty; the ignorance and

147

prejudice that permeate its power-structure; and, above all, the widespread vulgarity of its ideals and style of life. And Marcuse has grasped a truth that is of capital importance for any one who wants to change all this: the familiar incentives—higher wages, shorter hours, generally improved conditions of life—will no longer induce the proletariat to revolt, since the productive efficiency of 'corporate capitalism' has so enriched and (Marcuse would say) corrupted the workers that they have become integrated with, and reconciled to, the system that he wants them to help him to destroy.

What, then, does Marcuse propose to do about it? Reform by means of constitutional methods is no longer possible: the authorities have an automatic, built-in majority. As for a full-scale sanguinary revolution, he would not shrink from that; but he recognises that it would be very difficult today, at any rate in the United States, to organise a revolution successfully; the forces of capitalism are too strongly entrenched. What he recommends, therefore, is a perpetual guerrilla warfare against the powers that be in every department of the national life, a persistent campaign intended to erode the foundations of American culture, so that its structure will disintegrate or become top-heavy and collapse. The whole system is in his opinion a sham: 'freedom' and 'democracy', 'law' and 'order', 'decency' and 'art', have become for him 'dirty' words, the things they stand for in America today are all of them subjected to his vitriolic attack. All methods of carrying on warfare against them are legitimate, violent and non-violent alike.

Marcuse calls upon his young 'non-conformist' followers to effect a 'methodical desublimation of traditional culture' by means of 'counter-violence', 'direct action', and 'uncivil disobedience' in every sphere of life. This social sabotage is to be directed 'against the beautiful in [the established] culture, against its all too sublimated, segregated, orderly, harmonising forms'. So he is all in favour of anti-art (pending the complete abolition of art by its absorption into life), together with 'black music (and its avant-gardistic white equivalent)', and he approves of drug-taking—the 'trip', he says 'involves the dissolution of the ego shaped by the established society'—and of the atmosphere in which, as he puts it, 'the hatred of the young bursts into laughter and song, mixing the barricade and the dance-floor, love play and heroism' (so the Penguin text: perhaps a misprint for 'heroin'?). He recommends 'the methodical use of obscenities', as practised by 'black and white radicals', in order to effect 'a methodical subversion of the linguistic universe of the establishment'; President X and Governor Y, he says,

149

should be called 'pig X' and pig Y' and addressed as 'mother fuckers', because they are 'men who have perpetrated the unspeakable Oedipal crime'. He approves not only of dirty language, but of dirty bodies, welcoming what he calls 'the erotic belligerency in the songs of protest, the sensuousness of long hair, of the body unsoiled by plastic cleanliness'.

One recognises that this programme of action ministers to a deep, subliminal 'urge' on the part of Marcuse and those who feel as he does; but one can't help wondering what positive end they hope to achieve by putting it into practice, beyond the satisfaction of their own vindictiveness. What alternative to the existing system have they to offer? 'A free society, is Marcuse's answer. But what is a free society, and how is it to be established? These are vital questions; but anyone who searches this *Essay* for a satisfactory—or even an intelligible—answer to them will search in vain: whenever the Professor comes within a mile of them he emits a smoke-screen of semi-philosophical, semi-psychological, jargon. This is the nearest he can get to a definition of a 'free society':

'The advent of a free society would be characterized by the fact that the growth of well-being turns into an essentially new quality of life. This qualitative change must occur in the needs, in the infrastructure of man (itself a dimension of the infrastructure of society). . . . Such a change would constitute the instinctual basis for freedom which the long history of class society has blocked. Freedom would become the environment of an organism which is no longer capable of adapting to the competitive performances required for well-being under domination.'

On the principle, presumably, of *obscurum per obscurius*, Marcuse goes on to explain that 'the rebellion would have taken root in the very nature, the "biology" of the individual; and on these new grounds, the rebels would redefine the objectives and the strategy of the political struggle, in which alone the concrete goals of liberation can be determined.'

In his first chapter Marcuse describes the 'biological transformation' that provides the necessary foundation for his 'new society':

'The construction of such a society . . . presupposes a type of man with a different sensitivity as well as consciousness: men who would speak a different language, have different gestures, follow different impulses. . . . The imagination of such men and women would fashion their reason and tend to make the process of production a process of creation. This is the utopian concept of socialism which envisages the ingression of freedom into the realm of necessity, and the union

151

between causality by necessity and causality by freedom.'

This 'utopian' concept of a change in human nature, he says, can be realized here and now; in his second chapter, 'The New Sensibility,' he gets down to brass tacks, or as near brass tacks as he is capable of getting, and tells us how it will be effected:

'Technique . . . assuming the features of art, would translate subjective sensibility into objective form, into reality. This would be the sensibility of men and women who do not have to be ashamed of themselves any more because they have overcome the sense of guilt . . . who are physiologically and psychologically able to experience things, and each other, outside the context of violence and exploitation. The new sensibility has become, by this very token, *praxis*.'

Let us assume that all this makes sense, that Marcuse's 'biological transformation' has taken place, and that his 'free society' has replaced the 'exploitative society' of today. How will that society work? Will there be laws—and who will enforce them? Will there be motor-cars—and who will make them? Will there be a monetary system, and wages? How will the hospitals be kept going? Will this 'free society' be international? If not, how will the free nation maintain itself against its 'exploitative' rivals?

152

To such questions Professor Marcuse simply has no answer, and he admits it:

'What kind of life? . . . The demand is meaningless if it asks for a blueprint of the specific institutions and relationships which would be those of this new society: they cannot be determined *a priori*; they will develop, in trial and error, as the new society develops. . . . The possibilities of the new society are sufficiently "abstract"—i.e. removed from and incongruous with the established universe—to defy any attempt to identify them in the terms of this universe'.

All this, of course, is sheer Evangelism. Professor Marcuse's 'biological transformation' is simply the regeneration of man, his 'free society' is no more and no less than the Kingdom of Heaven, his gospel is the gospel of the early Christian millenarian. True, the early Christians did manage to transform the Roman Empire from within, but what chance of a similar success would Christianity have if someone tried to start it up again today? Mankind was successfully inoculated with that serum nearly two thousand years ago and western industrial civilization today has tougher defences than the Empire of Severus.

Marcuse, plainly, is what Yeats called an old bellows full of angry wind; but it would be wrong to suppose that his practical importance is proportionate to the intrinsic value of his ideas; he might

153

yet blow widespread embers into flame. He is an idol and an oracle for youthful rebels all over the world; his millenarian gospel makes a natural appeal to adolescent idealists; his polysyllabic philosophising is calculated to impress the intellectually immature; his hatreds coincide with the hatreds of the student Left. Not only that: in this country he has been adopted by people who should (and perhaps really do) see through him: *New Society*, for instance, says of his philosophy that 'its importance for the development of sociology . . . is difficult to underrate'—a left-handed (New Left-handed?) compliment, it is true, but still, I suppose, a compliment—while the Educational Supplement of *The Times* finds that 'what is impressive about Marcuse's writing is not simply its depth, but also its compassion and virtuosity'.

Virtuosity! I should have thought it impossible to praise Professor Marcuse's prose style except in jest; and as for compassion, perhaps the most remarkable feature of his book is the inhumanity that permeates it; the malevolence with which the author assails his enemies is so indiscriminate and so extreme as to seem at times insincere and mechanical; even his approval of the young rebels is not tinged by human feeling; he evidently thinks about people in categories. There is something Germanic about this, as there is about Marcuse's lack of humour and his pretentious abstractions. Germanic, too, is the note of sentiment on which the last essay closes, where the Professor tries to touch our hearts by quoting from a 'young black girl'. Unfortunately the young black girl—whose existence one may be permitted to doubt—turns out to be no more worth listening to than the old white man.

All in all, this is, I think, the *nastiest* book that I have ever read.

Beards

One of the most remarkable things that have happened in this country during the past twenty years or so—and I believe the same phenomenon has presented itself on the Continent and in the United States—is the outbreak, the growth and the spread of beards among the younger generation.

When I was a child—that is now fifty or sixty years ago—a beard was something that was very rarely to be seen, at any rate in this country. In those days, the beard was a badge of authority and age: it conferred venerability upon the man who wore it. If you were a child then, you associated beards with Old Testament figures—with God the Father and the Major Prophets—and with Father Christmas, and perhaps with your own grandfather. They inspired reverence—or, if you were a naughty child, they invited irreverence. There was the game—I wonder if anyone remembers it today?—of 'Beaver'. It wasn't really a game; it was a sort of childish prank that had a brief spell of popularity: if a small boy saw a bearded figure approaching him in the street, he would wait until the old gentleman got quite close, and then run past him, crying out 'BEAVER!', and leaving his victim in a state of bearded bewilderment. (A child would have a busy time today, if when he walked in the street, he had to call out 'Beaver' every time he was confronted with a beard).

In those days of my childhood, most beards, it seemed, were white. But there were other, darker beards—less venerable, perhaps, but still conveying a sense of dignity and authority. The two successive monarchs of the time, King Edward VII and King George V, both wore trim brown beards, which you could see every day on the coinage and on postage stamps. (I can see these stamps now in my mind's eye: the green halfpenny one for postcards and the red penny one for letters. We have progressed a long way since then!) Anyhow, the beard—white or brown, neat or bushy—was something rare, something remote, something special, associated always with authority or age.

And so it remained, until the last War—which was a dividing line, a water-shed, in this as in so many other aspects of social life.

Before I consider the latest development in this field—the recent, post-War springing and sprouting and spreading of the beard—let us take a look back over the more distant past. I am no historian,

157

but I think I am right in saying that there have been two beardless Western cultures; there may have been more, but these two stand out in my mind: the culture of the late Roman Republic and early Roman Empire, and the society of England and Western Europe in the eighteenth century.

For several hundred years, about the beginning of the Christian era, the clean-shaven Romans were the guardians of Western civilization, keeping at bay the bearded barbarians, the shaggy savages who hemmed them in on every side. Indeed, it's tempting to derive the word 'barbarian' from the latin *barba*, a beard; to equate *barbari* (the barbarians) with *barbati* (the wearers of beards), and to suggest that it was from their beards that the barbarians derived their name. I am afraid the dictionary won't allow that derivation, but I think that a child in a Roman nursery might have been forgiven for making the mistake.

Anyhow, with the fall of the Roman Empire, the beard came into its own, and for more than a thousand years, through the Dark Ages and the Middle Ages, you must think of Europe under the domination of the beard; with only the monasteries providing a refuge for the clean-shaven. Even the Renaissance brought no respite—only a change of fashion. The Tudors and Stuarts trimmed their beards, and set them off with a ruff.

The second clean-shaven culture was that of

Western Europe in, roughly speaking, the eighteenth century. It was a culture that started—at any rate here in Britain—in the late seventeenth century and lasted on until nearly the middle of the nineteenth. For about a hundred and fifty years, it would be practically true to say, *not a beard grew upon an English chin*. Review the roll of English monarchs, statesmen, churchmen, lawyers, men of letters, poets, artists, from the Restoration in 1660 to the accession of Queen Victoria in 1837, summon up their faces before your mind's eye— Steele and Addison, Pope and Swift, Gray and Collins, Fielding and Sterne, Gibbon, Doctor Johnson, Burke, Blackstone, Lord Mansfield, Lord Eldon, the elder and the younger Pitt, Cowper, Crabbe, Sir Walter Scott—there is not a bearded face among them: they are clean-shaven to a man. Then, at the turn of the century, came the Romantics, with their revolt against convention, their return to Nature—among them you might have expected an outbreak of the beard—but not a bit of it! Byron, Shelley, Keats, Coleridge, Wordsworth—all of them had smooth, clear, clean complexions, with shaven cheeks and chins. Even William Blake, in almost every aspect of life a rebel against the customs and conventions of his age, even Blake was in this respect a conformist.

Then, just before the middle of the nineteenth

century, a change came over the face of England: whiskers began to sprout upon it. What was the reason for the change—or, reason apart, what was the cause of it? I don't know. I've heard it suggested that it lay in the Crimea: that the rigours of the Crimean winter made it impossible for the troops to shave, and that the returning war-heroes set a fashion that was generally adopted by their countrymen. I haven't tried to verify this; and I must say that to me, it doesn't sound very plausible. For one thing, the change seems to have set in earlier than the mid-fifties, the date of the Crimean War. To judge from the pictures in *Punch* (which throws a flood of light upon the social history of the time), I should say that the fashion was already creeping in in the 1840s.

However that may be, it is true that by the 1860's the beard and the whisker dominated, in more senses than one, the face of England: the mid-Victorian age was the flowering-time of hair on the English cheek and chin. When I complain about the contemporary outcrop of beards and whiskers, people say to me 'But think of the Victorians, whom you so much admire! Think of Dickens and Darwin, Tennyson and Browning! Surely they reconcile you to the idea of the beard?' Well! it isn't clear to me why I should be expected to tolerate something, and still less clear why I should be expected to like it, just because it was tolerated, or approved of, by the Victorians. And I can only say that one of the reasons why I am glad that I didn't live in the Victorian age is that if I had, I am sure I should have felt myself entangled and suffocated by the over-growth of beard and whisker on the faces of those around me. Living in the twentieth century, at least one is spared that—or was spared it until the recent recrudescense of the hirsute and the hispid which is the occasion of this talk. And there is a more telling reply to people who try to reconcile one to the beard by referring to 'Eminent Victorians' like Tennyson and Browning, Dickens and Darwin. Have they ever compared the familiar portraits of those great men in their maturity and old age with the portraits that show what they looked like when they were young? Look, for instance, at Maclise's drawings of the youthful Dickens or Samuel Laurence's marvellous oil-sketch of Tennyson as a young man of thirty, and you will see what a tragedy it was that they smothered the contours of cheek and lips with the bush of beard and whisker that hid their beauty for the better part of their lives and created the image by which they are known to posterity.

Well! After half-a-century or so of hispidity, the beard went out, in this country at any rate, as swiftly and completely as it had come in. It remained, I think, in fashion in France and other Latin countries. The French Master in my school-days was traditionally a bearded figure. Its disappearance in England is very easily explained: it was surely due to the invention at the turn of the century, of the safety-razor—I should say the most beneficial—and the only entirely beneficial scientific invention of all time. Let me take this opportunity of paying a public tribute to the two great G-men—an American and a Frenchman, Kingsley Gillette and Joseph Guillotin—the two eponymous heroes of the cutting blade. The one provided a speedy and painless end for those who had to die upon the scaffold; the other, a comfort enjoyed by the ordinary citizen every morning of his life. So we reached that happy time, the early days of this present century, the days of my childhood, which I recalled at the beginning of this talk, when beards were few and far between and were recognized, as I said, as symbols of authority.

Of course, there were, even in those days, a few so to speak *unlicensed* beards; there were eccentrics who 'sported' a beard, like Bernard Shaw, whose beard was a sort of theatrical property, and characters like D. H. Lawrence, whose beard was the outward and visible sign of his dominant masculinity. They were the exceptions that proved the rule. The rule prevailed, as I have said, until

162

the last War, and for perhaps a decade beyond it. Then, in the fifties, it was silently, swiftly and universally repealed—at least among the younger generation.

The best place for observing a change in the habits of the young is a university town, where the streets, in term-time, are thronged by a student population. For twenty-five years, from 1952, I lived in a house with windows overlooking the High Street of Oxford. It was an ideal vantage point for observing the student youth of England and their changing life-style. I can only say that the alteration that has come over the outward appearance of the average student during that period is phenomenal—and in my opinion, horrifying. Shock-headed and dishevelled, with hair that seems to have run to seed, hiding neck and ears in a whiskery overgrowth, they pad along the city pavements in patched and dirty jeans. Of course, there are exceptions, many and honourable exceptions; but I am speaking of the prevailing, indeed, the almost universal, type. This change is phenomenal in two senses: as a transformation, it is remarkable; and it is also, surely, the outward sign of an inner disposition. The most remarkable feature of this change in life-style is the growth of beards and whiskers on the chins and cheeks of the young men.

Why do they grow beards? Not in imitation of

their elders—their elders, as I've said, are but rarely bearded. Nor in order to look grown-up, or older than they really are. Nor, I think, as a proof of manliness—for the beard is often associated with long hair, straight or in curls, over the wearer's shoulder, like a girl's. 'It's years,' said an Oxford friend of mine the other day—and he said it with a sigh—'It's years since I've seen the back of a young man's neck.' Nor do they do it in order to be different from, or to shock, their elders. I think it goes deeper than that. They are protesting not merely against middle-class respectability, or against a particular sort of convention, but against all conventions alike; not against one class, but against the whole structure of society. They are not concerned with appearances, they are concerned in a more serious sense, about the hypocrisy of a society that is itself so much concerned with appearances. They are giving the world a visual lesson in priorities: in a word, they are on the way back to Nature, and the types they personify are the noble savage and the wild man of the woods.

I think that the girls have a certain responsibility in this matter. If they don't actually encourage it, they could surely put a stop to it if they really wanted to. I recall an incident that happened to me not so very long ago. I had been walking in the High Street with a young friend of mine and we stopped at a corner where our ways parted. I took my courage in both hands and said what I had been wanting to say for a long time, but hadn't dared to take the plunge. 'Do you mind if I say something personal? Don't take offence! It's about your beard.' And in a few halting sentences I tried to tell him that I thought that by growing his beard he was spoiling what would otherwise have been a most attractive face. Before he could answer, we were interrupted by the arrival of a third party—his girl-friend, whom I didn't know. We were introduced. 'I hope I'm not interrupting your conversation,' she said. I explained what I had been saying and appealed to her for support. Surely in her I should find an ally? My hope was a vain one. Even while I spoke I could see her looking up at him with the eyes of a worshipper: 'His beard? But I adore it!' she said—and I realized that my cause was a lost one.

Well! you can't argue against that. And I don't care to speculate about it, either. But I find it hard to believe that the young men increase their attractiveness to the other sex by growing hair upon their chins, or that that is their reason for growing it. We have been told by Kipling—or by one of his characters—that being kissed by a man who doesn't wax his moustache is like eating an egg without salt. It may be. But, moustache or no moustache, I can't believe that the sensuous quality of an embrace is enhanced by hair upon the chin.

Well! I don't want to pass judgment on the new life-style of the young in general nor, in particular, on the proliferation of the beard that is such a prominent feature of that life-style. But I must register my reaction to it, which is a profound antipathy. On what is that antipathy based? It must, I think, be something very deep down in me, something I can't analyse. I like order, and seemliness, and decency; I like the clean, the neat, the smooth, the comely. I attach great importance to outward appearances. I remember as a child how I enjoyed the sound of the lawn-mower and loved to see the smooth green surface that it left behind it. I used to watch with fascination the gardener trimming the hedge with his shears; and I remember begging, when I stayed with my grandmother, to be allowed to go to the stables and see the carriage-horses being clipped.

My first razor was a treasure, my first shave an infinitely satisfying experience. And I well remember the War, when as a private soldier I was sent to a Cadet Training Unit to be turned into an officer (which I didn't at all want to be), how I dreaded being told that if I was commissioned I should have to wear a moustache. I should certainly have jibbed at that: I just couldn't have done it. Fortunately or unfortunately, I didn't have to: a moustache was no longer required for commissioned rank. But I remember lying awake on my bed in the barrack-room, surrounded by my fellow-cadets, all eager to become moustachio-ed subalterns: and how, as I lay there in the dark, I seemed to hear the hair growing on their upper lips.

And one of the things—one among many others—that made the Bar to me a delightful profession, was the fact that it was a clean shaven profession. During twenty years of practice in the Courts, I remember only one bearded barrister (the famous Serjeant Sullivan) and one Judge who was bearded and one who wore a moustache—they were the exceptions that proved the rule. Well! I deplore the outbreak of the hispid and the hirsute that marks the younger generation today. But there is nothing I can do about it.

What of the future? I confess that I see no signs of any improvement, no indications of an impending change. I sometimes talk about it to the older generation, to the parents of bearded sons. And, of course, they are traitors: the parents have sold the pass, they have gone over to the other side. What do they say? It's always the same thing: 'Oh, there are fewer beards today, I'm certain! And as for long hair, the fashion for it has quite gone out. You don't see half as many of them about nowadays.' I am so tired of having

167

this said to me! Mothers and fathers of the bearded—particularly mothers—have been saying it to me year after year—and every year the situation seems to me to be exactly the same—no worse, perhaps, but certainly no better.

Then I strike nearer home, and ask about the beard on the chin of their son, Timothy: what do they think of that? It's always the same story: 'At first we weren't quite sure about it; but he knew what he wanted, and felt certain it was what his face *needed*, and he was right all along! We wouldn't have him without it for the world!' To that, I have nothing to say. And after a minute or two's silence, the mother goes on, betraying, although she doesn't know it, her real feelings: 'And anyhow, it'll be all right in a year or two: he'll take it off, I'm sure, when he goes down from the university.' What can one reply to that? Silence is the only comment, and into silence I relapse.

Too Much of a Good Thing

The three pieces that follow are the fruits of an invitation from the Committee on Social Thought of the University of Chicago, who asked me to deliver the Sara Halle Schaffner Lectures at the University in 1976. When extending their invitation, the Committee gave me a wide discretion as to the topics I might take for my lectures, stipulating only that my theme should be one that lay within the field indicated by the title Social Thought.

This presented me with a problem: how should I interpret 'Social Thought'? I took it to mean reflections about society, about the world in which we live together, and I imagined that I had been asked, 'What do you think about the way the world is going? What do you see as being the most significant, the most important, tendencies of the age? What do you feel about them?' My answers to these questions consisted, as the following pages will show, simply of my own reflections. I am not a philosopher, nor a sociologist, nor a politician; I have no theory to expound, no principles to enunciate, no cause to advocate: all I

169

have to offer is my personal impressions, my personal reactions. I have tried to analyze them and to sort them out, but they remain essentially personal, my own account of what seem to me to be the most significant tendencies of the age.

What do I mean by 'the age'? I mean the period, just over a human generation, that has elapsed since the end of the Second World War. I cannot help contrasting the old days with today; 'the old days' for me means 'before the War'; 'today' means 'since the War.' This isn't just a convenient chronological division, like the turn of a century; the War didn't only divide the pre-War from the post-War world; it helped to change the pre-War into the post-War world. Each of the succeeding decades, the fifties, the sixties, the seventies, may have contributed distinguishable waves, perhaps even cross-currents, of its own; but over the whole period a new tide, I think, has set in.

I must place 'the age' in space as well as time, for when one speaks of 'the tendencies of the age,' one must be thinking of a particular society, or particular societies, in which the tendencies manifest themselves. The suggestions I have to offer are based on my own observation of what is happening in my own country, and on what, so far as I can judge, is happening in other countries in Western Europe.

What then are the significant tendencies that

have shown themselves in Great Britain since the end of the Second World War? I think they are tendencies towards increased liberty, increased equality, and increased humanity. As my main title indicates, I think that all these tendencies are good things, but that it is possible for them to go too far. In the chapters that follow, I try to explain what I mean by 'going too far' in regard to each of them.

Equality

Equality, Humanity, Liberty—it sounds like the French Revolution! But the tendencies towards increased equality, increased humanity, increased liberty, that I observe making themselves felt, at any rate in my own country, do not operate, or so it seems to me, in a political or an economic context. If you compare Britain today with Britain as it was in the 1920s and the 1930s, you have to conclude that by and large in the political and economic fields the battle for liberty and equality has been won. When I was a boy, organized labour was practically unrepresented

171

in Parliament. There was a rudimentary Labour Party, with less, I think, than a dozen seats in the House of Commons. Power was shared between the Conservatives and the Liberals, both of which parties consisted almost entirely of members who were drawn from, and represented, the governing class. After the First World War, things changed quickly: the first Labour government in England took office in 1924, the year before my freshman's year at Oxford. Since the Second World War, the Liberal Party has almost disappeared, and power has been shared between Labour and Conservatives. Labour has always been the party of the Left, the majority of the working class, with a strong infusion of intellectuals; the Conservatives have been the party of the Right, the propertied and the professional classes, with an infusion of the aristocracy and the support of about a quarter of the working class. But today there is less to distinguish the Labour Party from the Conservatives, whether in their composition or in their policies, than there was to distinguish the Liberals from the Conservatives in the old days. There is no longer a governing class: those who in effect govern the country are no longer identifiable with any social stratum. The most obvious difference in policy between the political parties, a cynic might say, is that the Labour Party offers higher bribes to the Trade

Unions than do the Conservatives.

As for economic equality, there are still rich and poor today in Great Britain, though not so many very rich as in the pre-War world, and far fewer very poor. The gap between the two is being perpetually reduced by increasingly heavy taxation on the one hand, and ever-rising wages and a lavish provision of 'Public Welfare' on the other.

Finally, social equality. Britain is still, I suppose, a class-ridden society compared with the United States.* I can only say that compared with the Britain of the old days, society in Britain today is practically classless, You may recall Matthew Arnold's essay on Equality, published almost exactly a hundred years ago, in his *Mixed Essays* (1879). In that essay Arnold, taking for his text the maxim 'Choose Equality,' contrasts the English love of inequality with the passion for equality that has always characterized the French. France, he declared, was the most civilized of nations, and it was to her passion for equality that she owed that pre-eminence. England, compared with France, was uncivilized, and that was because English society was rigidly stratified in three social orders, which he called 'our

---

* 'The lower classes' is a phrase no longer in use; but (anomalously) the phrase 'the middle classes' and even the adjective 'upper-class' (whence the colloquial 'U' and 'non-U') are still current; and the word 'gentleman' retains a social connotation that is well understood, if difficult to explain.

eternal trio'—the Barbarians (the aristocracy), the Philistines (the middle class), and the Populace. England, in Arnold's view, would never become a truly civilized country until the hierarchy was abolished. The best and quickest way to abolish it, he thought, was to reform the law of inheritance in conformity with the Continental model, so that great landed estates, or large accumulations of property, should be broken up and redistributed with each succeeding generation.

It wasn't until after Arnold's death that the first step was taken. The Finance Act of 1894 introduced Estate Duty, a levy on inheritance which almost revolutionized the existing system of taxation. When an estate changed ownership on a death, a fraction of it, calculated at a rate determined by its total value, was to be confiscated by the State. The effect of Death Duties, which have now reached crippling proportions, of ever-rising taxes on income, and of vast increases in wages and in expenditure on Public Welfare and on State education—to which causes one must add the levelling and unifying influence of the 'mass media'—has been to bring about during the present century, in large measure, the social equalization that Arnold so much desired.

Since the end of the last war one may say that there are in Britain practically speaking only two classes—a large and diversified middle class and a
174

large and diversified working class—and the social and economic gap between the two is being steadily diminished.

In short, during the hundred years that have elapsed since Arnold published his essay on Equality, Great Britain, assisted by two World Wars, has carried out a bloodless political and social revolution, and is well on the way towards becoming an egalitarian society. If that is so, how—you may ask—can I say that the most significant tendencies of today, as compared with what I have called the old days, include pressures for increased liberty and equality? Hasn't the battle been won already? Where do we go from here?

My answer is that the tendencies I am talking about are concerned not with political but with personal relationships—not with relations between the individual and the State, or between groups, or between citizen and citizen, but with relations between human beings as human beings. Of course I am not denying that there are real political revolutionaries in Britain—people who are so hostile to 'bourgeois' society, and so impatient of 'consensus' government and 'repressive tolerance,' that they would like to blow the whole Establishment sky-high. That is the professed aim of the Communist Party of Great Britain and of a miscellaneous crew of Marxists

175

and Maoists, operating for the most part unorganized and underground. They are negligible in numbers and their influence doesn't amount, I should say, to a 'significant tendency.' But, apart from such dedicated extremists, there are very many, especially among the younger generation, who, without, being politically minded or interested in revolutionary solutions, share the revolutionaries' hostility to the Establishment and their sense of alienation and personal frustration.

For the people I have in mind, equality, humanity, and liberty are not political or economic concepts. Equality is not an ideal to be realized by the overthrow of a governing class; it simply means that all hierarchies are unnatural, that no man is really good enough to claim superiority, as a human being, to any other man.

Their humanity is inspired not by any abstract theory of the Brotherhood of Man, but by natural compassion, by an innate reluctance to inflict suffering on any fellow creature. As for liberty, they think of it simply as the individual's right to unrestrained self-expression, the right to 'be yourself,' to 'do your own thing.'

If one wants to see a realization of these ideals, one should look not to the Communist state, but to the hippy commune. Hippy communes are not a frequent feature of the English scene; it is not a national characteristic to carry things to extremes.

But the ideals that inspire such a commune are shared and advocated—though not always consciously shared or explicitly advocated—by many of the younger generation in Britain today.

The younger generation! One of the things that differentiate the Britain of today from the Britain of yesterday is the prominence of the part now played on the national scene by the young, and the importance attached to what young people think, and what they say, and what they want.

What are the agencies that have brought about this increase in the prestige of the young? The process begins in the home and continues at school. First, the tendency towards increased humanity makes parents reluctant to impose their authority by force. In the old days disobedient children were punished by their parents, or by their nurses (today there are no longer nurses and nurseries: children live in close and continuous contact with their parents, and that itself is a social change of no small importance); today there is a revulsion against the very thought of punishment. Besides this, there are new theories, favoured by educational psychologists, about the bringing up of children. Children, it is said, should be treated as reasonable beings; you must not give an order or state a fact without providing an explanation. 'Because I say so'—words which in my youth seemed ample justification for a

177

parental command—are never heard in England today, and the very word 'obedience' has a sadly old-fashioned ring. Again, parents themselves, if their authority is challenged, are often at a loss to justify it. They no longer themselves believe in the foundations on which it is supposed to rest, and—partly out of natural honesty, and partly because educationists tell them that it is wrong to deceive a child—they won't put forward justifications that they don't themselves believe in. Things were very different in the old days. My father, I remember, taught me the Catechism and the Ten Commandments. I don't think he really believed in the authority of the Church, or of the Scriptures, but I never thought of challenging him on the matter, and anyhow the Commandments and all they stood for provided a sort of framework that helped to keep me in my place.

Schoolmasters and university authorities today adopt the same humanitarian, egalitarian attitude as parents. Teaching and learning ought, we are told, to be looked on as a joint enterprise; the old-fashioned attitude of the university teacher, who not only instructed his pupils but cared for them and looked after them, is written off as 'paternalism': 'Don't speak of us as adolescents,' said an indignant student in Oxford the other day, 'we are *young adults*.' When they leave school or university, the young today are faced by no shortage of employment, and are no longer dependent economically upon their parents—'I shall cut you off with a shilling', 'I shall turn you out of the house', are no longer threats with any force behind them.*

All this has given the young in Britain a collective self-consciousness, a sense of solidarity, and has promoted them to be, I won't say a power in the land, but a sort of Fourth Estate. And it is among the younger generation that you will see most clearly at work the tendencies that I suggest are among the most significant features of society in Britain today, the tendencies that you will see worked out to their extreme in a community of hippies.

The tendencies I am talking about are expressed in the life-style nowadays adopted by the young in universities in Britain, and not only in universities. Let me give you the results of my own personal observation. I came back from London some twenty-five years ago, to live in Oxford. My windows look out on the High Street, the main thoroughfare of the city, thronged every day during term-time with students hurrying to and from lectures or strolling at ease with their friends during hours of leisure. The change that has come

* In England now, however, the 'job market' is said to be shrinking, and graduates are beginning to suffer from the general shortage of employment.

over the outward appearance of these young people during the last ten or fifteen years is phenomenal. When I say 'phenomenal' I mean phenomenal in two senses: it is a remarkable, an almost incredible, transformation, and it is also an outward sign of an inner disposition. In the old days, the Oxford student presented the classic image of youth, clean-limbed and fresh-complexioned, decent in dress and graceful in bearing. Today, his place has been taken by a new breed of adolescent, shock-headed and dishevelled, with hair that seems to have run to seed, hiding ears and neck in a whiskery over-growth. Clad in patched jeans and dirty anoraks, they pad hand in hand, sometimes with bare feet, along the city pavements, horrible specimens of humanity. Of course, not all the young are like that; but that is, and has been for the last decade or so, an all too familiar image.

What is it that impels so many decent, intelligent, and (no doubt) potentially attractive young people to cultivate the hirsute and the hispid, the scruffy and the unkempt, and to present such a loathsome exterior to each other and to the world at large?

Most of the young in Oxford, no doubt, if you asked them why they cultivated the uncouth, would be hard put to it to suggest a reason: they do it because the others do. But what was it that determined the trend, and what sustains it? Of course it is a challenge to bourgeois respectability, the 'square,' the conventional, the dark blue suit, the carefully rolled umbrella. But why does the challenge take this form? Why not extravagant eccentric elegance, like the æsthetes of the 1880s challenging Victorian conventionality? Plainly, the challenge of these young people goes deeper: they are protesting—whether they know it or not—not merely against middle-class respectability, against a particular sort of convention, but against all conventions alike; not against one class, but against the whole structure of society; they are not concerned with appearances, they are concerned, in a more serious sense, about the hypocrisy of a society that is itself so much concerned with appearances. 'We attach,' they are saying, 'more importance to the purity of our motives and the nobility of our ideals than to the cleanliness of our bodies and the neatness of our clothes. We are giving the world a visual lesson in priorities.' And it is significant that the types they personify, with their straggling locks, their bushy beards, their bare feet, are the primitive man and the early Christian—Robinson Crusoe and Jesus Christ—the noble savage, the wild man of the woods, and the prophet whose Kingdom is not of this world.

I shall explore later on the effect of their libertarian and humanitarian feelings: here what I am concerned with is their feeling for equality.

Equality! It is a topic appropriate, surely, to the year that marks the bicentenary of the signing of the Declaration of Independence: the first of the truths enunciated by the Founding Fathers was that all men are created equal.

Confronted with this sublimely confident assertion, I can only ask 'What on earth does it mean? What did they think that it meant?' It is said to be self-evident. Well, it had better be—for surely there is no external evidence to support it. I cannot myself think of any sense of the word 'equal' that will make the proposition true. Men—which I take it includes in this context all human beings—differ from each other almost infinitely in physical and intellectual attributes and potentialities: it would be more plausible to say that it is undeniable that no two men are created equal.

The phrase 'created equal' seems to assume the existence of a Divine Creator. Indeed, the Declaration goes on to say expressly that their Creator endowed men with certain inalienable rights, of which it offers examples. 'Equal,' then, may be intended to mean equal in the sight of God: they are equal in His eyes, and in judging them He will treat them on a basis of absolute equality, in accordance with His own standards, whatever those

182

standards may be. This may be acceptable to people who believe in God, but it does not provide them with any guidance as to how they themselves are to regard, or to treat, their fellow men; and to people who don't believe in God, it is really no help at all.

What the authors of this famous sentence must surely have had in mind was not equality in the sight of God, but equality under the law of man—or, rather, equality by the law of man. I say '*by* the law' rather than '*under* the law,' because to say that men should be equal under the law is almost a tautology: of course every law must be administered strictly in accordance with its provisions and without respect of persons; so much is implied in calling it a law. It goes without saying that those who administer a law must treat all who come before them as that law says they should be treated, without favour or discrimination. The assertion must mean more than that: it must mean that men should be equal *by law*, that the law itself, the substantive law, should disregard men's natural inequalities and treat them as though they were in fact equal; it must not discriminate between them. What sort of discrimination is it that is forbidden? Plainly the law can impose different taxes on people by reference to the size of their incomes; plainly it can impose different conditions for work in different kinds of industry; plainly it may enjoin, or forbid, men to do things over which they have control, and may punish (or reward) them for having done such things. What the law must not do (the Founding Fathers may have been saying) is to discriminate between persons by reference to attributes over which they have no control, such as their age, their sex, their race. Perhaps, this was what the authors of the Declaration had in mind when they used the phrase '*created* equal'; they may have meant that the law should not discriminate between people by reference to attributes with which they were endowed by nature.

If that is what the proposition means, I can only ask, where are we to find the justification for it? Why, after all, should the laws of a country give equal rights to, and impose the same obligations on, lunatics and sane persons, children and adults, women and men, people of diverse races of nationalities? No religion, so far as I know, prescribes that the law shall treat these categories uniformly. To appeal to the rights of man is surely to beg the question: What are the rights of man? What are they based on? Natural law? What determines natural law? The general benefit of the community? But whether it benefits the community to give equal rights to these different categories is an empirical question.

Whatever they may have meant by their Declaration, it is instructive to observe how the Founding Fathers proceeded. Soon after drawing up the document, the men who signed it had to devise constitutions for the newly founded states. How far did they then put into practice the principle of equality so sublimely asserted in the Declaration? All men were created equal—yes! but slaves remained slaves, and slaves were excluded from the franchise, and along with slaves were excluded women, minors, servants, non-whites, Roman Catholics, and Jews.

In a recent lecture in Oxford, Professor J. P. Greene, of Johns Hopkins University, put forward an interesting explanation of this apparent contradiction of principle by practice. He suggested that the Founding Fathers, when they proclaimed the equality of man, were more concerned with the definition of man than the definition of equality. 'Equality' meant simply an equal share in electing the government: every qualified citizen must have a vote. The question was, who was to qualify as a citizen? Professor Greene argues most persuasively, and with an impressive array of supporting evidence from speeches and pamphlets by politicians and controversialists belonging to the period of the Revolution—that the signatories of the Declaration of Independence were perpetuating the laws concerning the franchise that their colonial forebears derived

185

from the mother country: to qualify as a voter under English law as it then stood, a man must have a stake in the country—he must have a property qualification—and he must be in a position to cast his vote without dependence upon others. Hence the exclusion of married women, of slaves, of servants, of infants (it probably was the practical truth in those days, that if you gave a vote to a woman or to a slave, you were simply giving an extra vote to the husband of the woman, or the owner of the slave) and also of Roman Catholics, who were thought to be subject to their spiritual directors. Besides this, the English law said, a man must be, in a special, civic sense, 'virtuous': he must enjoy not merely independence of others—owners, masters, husbands, parents—but mastery of self, freedom from internal subjection to his own passions. This criterion obviously excluded the insane and criminals; it was held also to exclude others who had such natural or cultural disabilities that they were incapable of self-control, and therefore lacked the capacity to attain the virtue and the competence that would qualify them for full civic status in society. Hence, I am sorry to say, it was felt necessary to exclude from the franchise not only slaves and married women, on the ground of their dependent status, but also, as lacking in the requisite civic competence, all women, even if unmarried, non-whites, even if free, and Jews.

So much for the political theories, or some of the political theories, that have actuated egalitarians in the past. My excursion into that field has been rapid and superficial; I embarked upon it only in order to point a contrast, a contrast between the political egalitarianism of yesterday and the very different and quite unpolitical egalitarianism that, if I am right, inspires many of the younger generation, and not only the younger generation, today. What they are concerned about is not political equality—'One man, one vote'—nor equality in the eye of the law—equal rights for unequal people. Such equalities do no more than organize and regulate the existing social and economic hierarchies, with the strong, astute, and the ambitious climbing to the top by the ladder of social mobility. They are not champions of the oppressed; they are simply reluctant to assert or to recognize the existence of superiority, they hate hierarchies, they abominate the conception of an élite. 'Meritocracy' is for them a dirty word—not because it is a horrible etymological hybrid, but because, like the word 'aristocracy,' it suggests a set of superior people. And the fact that 'meritocrats' achieve their superior position because they are lucky enough to have been endowed by nature with particular abilities or advantages makes matters no better—even if it

187

doesn't make them worse.

Few of those who are moved by this anti-hierarchical impulse have analysed it or thought out its implications. But it has a practical effect: one can see it at work in several fields.

First, in education: in schools and universities. There is, in England, an increasing body of opinion that is against publishing the results of examinations. If you publish examination results, it is said, you clearly advertise the superiority of the successful candidates and the inferiority of those who fail, and that humiliates the unsuccessful and is apt to give the successful swollen heads—and that must be bad for both alike. Even if the results are not published, the fact that candidates are graded is enough to register the painful contrast between success and failure, between superiority and inferiority; so it is proposed that examinations themselves should be abolished. Their abolition would not only make it more difficult to differentiate unkindly between one student and another, it would at the same time be a step towards abolishing the invidious distinction between the teacher and the taught. Invidious—for the process of learning is felt to be a co-operative endeavour, in which all should participate on an equal footing.

The huge and rapid extension of university education that has taken place in England since the War has led to applications from large numbers of less well qualified students for admission to the universities, and this in turn has led to pressure for lowering the standards for admission, and lowering the standards demanded for a degree. The standards must be shaped to the people, said a progressive don in Oxford the other day, rather than the people to the standards. The appeal was based on egalitarian and humanitarian grounds: it isn't the fault of the student if he is slower-witted than his rivals—moreover, he may not have enjoyed so good an education at school. Perhaps his parents couldn't afford to send him to a better school: should he be made to suffer for deficiencies that are no fault of his? Should a university cater for, and strive to produce, an academic élite? Should it not shape its standards so as to cater for the less fortunate of its students? My own answer to these questions would be unambiguous: I would say that being an élitist establishment is nothing to be ashamed of; excellence may not be a matter for pride, but it is never a matter for regret. Universities and schools that cast away their inheritance, not because they cease to believe in its value but out of deference to egalitarian pressure, are betraying an intellectual trust and becoming parties to the most recent manifestation of *la trahison des clercs*.

Besides education, there is another field in

which one can see at work the desire to suppress distinctions, and so to eliminate superiorities and inferiorities: that is, the field of Art. The very concept of Fine Art is as repugnant to the egalitarian as it is to the revolutionary: he abhors, and would repudiate, the sort of 'Civilization' that was the subject of a famous series of lectures by Lord Clark. The notorious pronouncement of John Lennon, the Beatle—'The Mona Lisa is a load of crap'—is relevant here: it should be interpreted, I think as expressing not a specific aesthetic judgment, but a desire to repudiate the traditional culture of the West and to reject in its totality the conception of Fine Art.

'Down with the past!' cries John Cage, the man who makes his music out of silence, 'Down with the masterpiece!' And from there it is a short step to 'Down with the artist!' The artist is a man with special gifts that can be fully appreciated only by the limited number of people who are born with, and have been able to cultivate, aesthetic sensibility and a special power of discrimination.

There was a significant dialogue between the poet Stephen Spender and a student rebel, when Spender was in Paris at the time of the rebellion in the Cité Universitaire of Nanterre. Spender asked the young rebel, meaning to be friendly, whether he was an artist. 'Am I an artist?' was the indignant reply, 'What do you mean? Everyone is an artist.' Yes, we are all artists now: hence 'audience participation' and Pop Art, the 'happening,' the *objet trouvé*, and the impersonal works of art produced by aleatory machines.

A similar tendency shows itself in the field of sex. Many of the young in Britain want, it seems, to mask the difference between male and female by putting into circulation as human currency a unisexual (but not hermaphroditic) type. A generation ago, it used to be said jokingly in Oxford that, what with men letting their hair grow long and women wearing trousers, soon you wouldn't be able to tell one sex from another. What was then said in jest has now become the sober truth. Every day one sees in the streets more and more young people with their hair about their shoulders, epicene in dress, and physically distinguishable as to sex only by profusion of beard on the one hand or, on the other, by protuberance of breast.

Why do they do it? Not just out of a desire for novelty, not simply in order to provoke their elders—that would be altogether too facile an explanation. Nor is it intended as a demonstration of their belief in equal rights for the two sexes. Whether they know it or not, the style has for them a purpose both more serious and more significant: by camouflaging the secondary differences between the sexes, it emphasizes their

191

common humanity.*

Sexual equality is taken for granted: what they are insisting upon is sexual indifference. It is a natural consequence of this depreciation of sexual difference that sexual activity itself should be for the young today a less serious and specialized affair than it was for their elders—less personal, less 'genital' (in current jargon) and more 'polymorphic,' an everyday incident, a recreation, like mixed hockey in the past, an activity that satisfies at the same time the desire for comradeship and the desire for play. Love, for them, means a diffused benevolence, which finds expression in altruistic concern for the 'alienated' and the oppressed, and also in the impersonal, half-mystical, love of the 'love-in,' a gathering where, as at the *agapai* of the early Christians, everybody enjoys a loving association, of one sort or another, with everybody else. The one thing that love does not mean to them, it seems, is the mysterious, possessive, devastating personal passion, known to the Greeks as *eros*, the intense preoccupation— a favourite theme of so many novelists and poets—of one individual person with another.

Too much of a good thing! It is surely a good thing that a new generation should grow up sincere,

---

* This is the feeling that inspires the chorus of the Unisex Anthem:
Raise the clarion call again:
Beards for women, breasts for men!

honest, humble, high-minded, compassionate, humane; opposed to the oppression of one class, or one race, by another, to hostility between nations, to the use of force, to war. Honesty, humility, compassion—are these really things that you can have too much of?

Well, yes: I think that you can have too much of them, in the sense that you can pay too dearly for their indulgence: you may find that by indulging in them without restraint you have sacrificed civilization itself. Civilization depends for its existence upon maintaining the authority of the law; the authority of the law cannot be maintained without the application of force—and force means suffering. Compassion is not enough.

Civilized society depends, likewise, upon the maintenance of a highly artificial system of conventions: 'Civilization,' said J. M. Keynes, 'is a thin and precarious crust erected by the personality and the will of a very few and only maintained by rules and conventions skilfully put across and guilefully preserved.' Not long ago I read a *graffito* inscribed upon an Oxford wall: 'Smash hypocrisy now!' was the message that is carried. But hypocrisy, in the sense intended by the author of that message, is the cement that holds society together: 'smash' hypocrisy and you destroy civilization. Honesty is not enough.

Finally, civilization depends upon the recognition

193

and the cultivation of excellence, and excellence implies superiority. Equality means the denial of superiority, and ultimately the denial of diversity, for every difference between one human being and another may be made the ground for asserting a superiority or an inferiority on one side or the other. Absolute equality between human beings, if it were attainable, would mean, as it does in the world of mathematics, absolute identity. Against such a conclusion even that egalitarian nation, the French, have lodged their protest: *Vive la différence!* And Matthew Arnold, if he saw the lengths to which his doctrine is being pressed today, would surely change his message and bid us 'Choose inequality!'

Humanity

There are, as it seems to me, several tendencies that make themselves felt in society today, in Great Britain and, I suspect, elsewhere in the West, that are undeniably good, but can be overvalued; if we pay too highly for them, I suggest, and if we let them carry us too far, the world will be a worse place. One of these tendencies is a tendency towards increased humanity.

When I use the word humanity, of course I don't mean the condition of being human; I mean the attribute of being humane—humaneness of disposition. Of course I think that it is a good thing that human beings should be humane, that they should be disposed to be kind and gentle to each other and to all living creatures, that they should shrink from imposing their wills by force upon their fellow men and from inflicting pain or injury upon them, and that they should seek to promote this disposition among human beings generally. Humanity in this sense is a good thing; it distinguishes us from brutes and barbarians, and the more successfully we cultivate our humane disposition, the less like brutes and barbarians we shall be.

Can we have too much of it? That is the question. When we are judging individuals, can we safely say the kinder, the gentler, the more humane a person is, the better he is as a member of society? And when we compare one society with another, can we say that the more humane it is in its customs and its laws, the better a society it is? I think that that would be to go too far. I think it would be to over-value one good thing at the expense of others. And I think that today, at least in Great Britain, we are in danger of doing just

195

that—indeed, that in certain areas we are doing it already.

It is a bad thing to be hard: but it does not follow that it is a good thing to be soft—and there are situations in which it is a good thing, a necessary thing, to be tough. A hard man is a man deficient in human sympathy; a tough man is a man who has his sympathy under control. It is toughness, not hardness, that I am contending for.

There are two reasons why our tender-heartedness needs to be supplemented by toughness. First, because someone who can't face the fact of suffering cannot adequately meet the responsibilities that fall to his lot as a member of society. Second, because—if it is judged by strictly practical and utilitarian tests, by its consequences, its effects upon society—the refusal to countenance the deliberate imposition of force and the deliberate infliction of pain may prove to be self-defeating: it may well produce a greater volume of suffering in the long run than it saves in the short run; in order to spare our mind's eye the image of immediate suffering, we may so act that others, and ourselves also, will suffer more in the end.

I said that a man who can't face the fact of suffering cannot meet his responsibilities as a member of society. Let me explain what I mean, and let me begin my explanation by offering you a very homely illustration.

I remember my mother telling me, after I was grown up, about a small boy who couldn't bear, in the nursery, to see or to think of his brother or his sisters being punished. He hated it so much that sometimes, when a misdemeanour of theirs was discovered, he would pretend that it was he that was the culprit: it really hurt him less if he himself was punished. Now these childish misdemeanours must have been very trivial, and the punishments far from severe, so the self-sacrifice of that small boy—if indeed it was self-sacrifice—wasn't very much to be proud of. But was it anything to be proud of at all? I ask the question with some concern, because I have to confess that I was that small boy myself; and I must say that I still shrink from the contemplation, even with the mind's eye, of somebody being hurt or humiliated. But wasn't my apparent altruism in my nursery days really a kind of selfishness or self-indulgence? The thing that worried me, was it really the suffering of my brother or my sisters? Was it not rather my own suffering at the thought of theirs? However that may have been, I was certainly giving more weight to my own feelings than to considerations of truth or—and here is the real point—of social justice and social good, of what was right and fair all round in the small world of the nursery.

That may give you a clue to what I mean when I say that a man who refuses to contemplate the infliction of pain, or the imposition of force, cannot meet his responsibilities as a member of society.

The man who allows himself to be guided entirely by the tenderness of his heart will not only decline to be himself a party to the imposition of force or the infliction of pain, he will oppose such imposition or infliction by others; and, if he is consistent, he will use his vote and his influence against laws and practices that involve the imposition of discipline by force. Such a man would find it impossible—surely—to run a prison, or a hospital, or a business, or a school, or indeed a family; and it is difficult to see how any of those institutions—or indeed any civilized society—could survive if the doctrines of pure humanitarianism were consistently applied. That is why I say that humanity, though a good thing, is a good thing of which you can have too much, and that a man who cannot face the fact of suffering cannot meet his responsibilities as a member of society.

And that leads me to my second reason for saying that tenderness must be supplemented by toughness: unalloyed, unrestrained humanity may well produce in the long run more suffering than it saves.

198

Let us look at some of the areas in which humanitarianism is put to the test. Take the issue of war and peace—or, rather, of war and pacifism. We prefer, surely, peace-loving nations to war-like, militaristic, nations; we abhor force as the arbiter of international disputes. We abhor it, but should we abjure it? Suppose two countries are threatened by a third, a totalitarian, militaristic power. One of the two, passively resisting, allows itself to be over-run; the other goes to war in its own defence. Do we applaud the first and deplore the second? In the country that goes to war, the individual citizen will, of course, be faced with a personal problem: is he, or is he not, to fight? Do we prefer the pacifist, the man who declines military service on conscientious grounds, or the man who joins the armed forces and takes his part in the bombing and destroying of the enemy? We may respect the pacifist, but should we conclude that the more pacifists there are in a nation, the more civilized that nation will be? By refusing to go to war, it may simply be signing its own death-warrant as a civilized society.

I suggested that there was in Britain today a pronounced, perhaps even an excessive, tendency towards increased humanity; I don't think that this applies, however, to the general attitude concerning war: I doubt whether the doctrine of pure pacifism has many adherents in the country.

199

The British have never been a militaristic nation, and people today are of course very conscious of the unspeakable horrors of modern warfare. They abolished peace-time National Military Service about twenty years ago, and I don't believe that any Government now would think of re-introducing it. Still, one may ask: 'If the country were faced with a clear threat of military aggression, could the Government depend on the response it would get if it declared war, mobilized the Army, and drafted civilians into it? Would there be, on any appreciable scale, a refusal to fight, a refusal to be drafted?' I don't think so. Memories of 1939, and the threat of Nazi invasion, and the Battle of Britain, are still potent, at least among older people—though when I talk to students who were born, as all today's students were, after the War was over, I sometimes wonder what would be their response to a call-up. 'Wouldn't you have joined up against Hitler?' I ask—and Hitler seems to be to them about as real a figure, about as much of a bogey-man, as Napoleon Bonaparte.

I have given you my opinion, for what it is worth, about the state of feeling in Great Britain. How it is with you over here, I do not know. I am not so rash as to invite discussion of the issues raised by the war from which this country has recently—shall I say?—rescued itself. Still less will I presume to pass judgment, one way or the other, upon any of those issues. But I can't help indulging in one speculation that arises from that war and that seems to me germane to the point that I am now trying to make. It is this. A vast majority of those who opposed the war, and a vast majority of those who declined to be drafted into the armed forces, must surely have been actuated by two convictions, right or wrong: first, that it was not a just war; and, second, that the country had never really been consulted on the question whether the war should be waged or not. So strongly, I imagine, were these convictions held by most of those concerned, that very few of them can have stayed to ask themselves the question 'Would I have take up arms and fought if I had thought the war to be a just one?', or the question 'Would I have been prepared to fight if I had thought it an unjust war, but it was the clear and declared opinion of the majority of the nation that it was a just war?' In short, the questions 'Is there such a thing as a just war?' and 'What makes a war a just war?' were questions that, in their view of the actual situation, simply did not arise.

And I would add this reflection: it may well be that the recent experience of this country has made it more likely that, if the question of going to war should again present itself in practice, the rising generation would answer: 'There is no such thing as a just war.' The experience that this country has been through has given war—so to speak—a bad name, and has strengthened the tendency to pure unadulterated pacifism. The humanitarian may say that this much good, at least, has come of evil: the rationalist, the tough-minded man, may not be so sure.

The problem I have so far put before you with regard to war is a straightforward one—in effect: 'Would you be a pacifist, or would you fight?' Let me add two special problems, where the issues are not so simple.

Suppose that you had been serving in the war against Hitler and that you held a prisoner who, to your knowledge, possessed information that would ensure and accelerate an Allied victory: to what lengths would you think it permissible to go in order to extract that information from him? Is there any form of torture, mental or physical, at which you would draw the line? Or suppose that just a touch of torture, a mild beating-up, would suffice; would you hold that even the slightest pressure was impermissible? Remember that if you don't extract the information, the war may continue for months or years, with hundreds of thousands of lives lost on both sides, and that it may end in victory for the Nazis. Assume also that all you did would be done in secret: no-one, or virtually no-one, need ever know about it. Faced by that problem, how should the true humanitarian act?

My other problem is a more topical one. It arises out of the activities of hijackers, who declare that, unless their demands are satisfied, they will kill the hostages that they have taken. Suppose that a hundred innocent persons are held captive, and threatened with death, unless half-a-dozen political prisoners are released. What attitude should be adopted by the Governments concerned? Are they to allow the innocent victims to be killed, perhaps one by one over a long and agonizing period, or are they to save their lives by fulfilling the hijackers' demands, however far-reaching and however outrageous? I do not suggest what the answer should be; but I cannot help pointing out that the extreme humanitarian in such a case would be in favour of saving the lives of the hostages, at whatever cost to the countries concerned, and to civilization generally.

Let me turn now to another field. The humanitarian tendency I have been speaking of reveals itself in the sphere of law-enforcement, and enforcement of discipline generally, especially in people's feelings about capital punishment and corporal punishment as sanctions under the criminal law, and about corporal punishment as a means of enforcing discipline in schools.

It is ten years since the death-penalty was abolished in Great Britain. I have taken part, during those years, in quite a number of debates, formal and informal, on the issue 'Should capital punishment be re-introduced?' and my experience is that it is difficult to find people, at any rate among academics and intellectuals, and especially among the younger generation, who will defend the death-penalty. During that period, crimes of violence, including murder, have dramatically increased, and I have no doubt that if a referendum of the whole population were taken, there would be a decisive majority in favour of restoring the death-penalty for murder and probably (but I am not so sure about this) a majority in favour of bringing back corporal punishment for particularly monstrous crimes of violence. But I am equally sure that no Government, whether Socialist or Conservative, will re-introduce either capital or corporal punishment in Great Britain.

You may ask why there is (if I am right) this divergence between the electorate as a whole and its representatives in Parliament. The answer, I think, is that on questions of social policy, Parliament is always, or almost always, in advance of the country at large; indeed it is a claim regularly made on behalf of the House of Commons that on such questions, it should, and does, give a lead to the nation; so it is not surprising that the humanitarian tendency that I detect among academics and intellectuals and the Left generally in England on the question of capital punishment should be reflected in the House of Commons, even though (if I am right) the mass of the people is not in agreement with them. The question, I suggest, is whether this is not an issue on which Parliament, pushed too far by a humanitarian tendency, is leading the country in the wrong direction.

I don't want to argue the case for or against capital punishment under English law, still less under American law, about which I know nothing, or next to nothing: Is it a cruel and unusual punishment? If it is recognized by the law, should it be mandatory? What are the requirements of due process?—on all such questions I am entirely ignorant. But capital punishment is a very topical issue, I gather, in the United States; it provides a test case, so to speak, for the humanitarian; and I should like to look at it, for a moment, not from the point of view of the lawyer, but from the point of view of the ordinary man.

The plea that is usually the first to be put forward by the opponents of capital punishment is an appeal to the sanctity of human life. 'Sanctity'— what does that mean? It has a religious ring. But what religion is being appealed to? Buddhism, I believe, regards *all* life, not merely human life, as sacred. But to those who are not Buddhists the religious appeal will surely ring hollow. Christianity, certainly, does not forbid the taking of human life—indeed, it teaches us that our earthly life is something on which we should not put too high a value. I suspect that when people appeal to the sanctity of human life in this context, all they really mean is that human life is a very valuable, a uniquely valuable, thing. No doubt it is. But whatever the value of a human life, two human lives must—other things being equal—be more valuable than one. Therefore, it must be right—other things, I repeat, being equal—to sacrifice one life to save two or more. And to save the lives of potential victims is one of the purposes of capital punishment. That leads to the question of deterrence.

Of course, one of the purposes of all criminal sanctions, one of the reasons for inflicting severe punishments upon delinquents, is that the punishment should deter other potential criminals from committing similar offences. And here I think that the horror and revulsion that makes sensitive, humane people want to abolish the death-penalty affords one of the strongest arguments for retaining it. For it *is* very horrible, dramatically horrible; and it is through this horror that it may act upon potential murderers. It operates at—so to speak—two levels.

206

Take the poisoner, or the bank-robber. Both plan their crimes. Both make calculations. And two principal factors in their calculations are: first, how likely it is that they will be caught; and, second, what will happen to them if they are. The thought that the punishment for murder is death may well be decisive in persuading the intending poisoner not to administer the arsenic, and the intending bank-robber not to carry a gun.

That is first-degree deterrence. By second-degree deterrence I mean the deterrent force of capital punishment operating, not by affecting the conscious thoughts of individuals tempted to kill, but by building up in the community, over a long period of time, a deep feeling of peculiar abhorrence for the crime of murder. I quote from the report of a Royal commission on Capital Punishment set up in England some years ago: 'This widely diffused effect on the moral consciousness of society is impossible to assess, but it must be at least as important as any direct part which the death penalty may play as a deterrent in the calculations of potential murderers.'

So much for first-degree and second-degree deterrence. Of course there are *crimes passionels*— murders that are committed in hot blood, under the influence of sudden overwhelming passion or of intoxication. In such cases, the murderer will not be affected, let alone deterred, by the thought

207

of the punishment to which his act renders him liable: he simply will not think about it. But that is only one category of murder; the cold-blooded murderer, on the other hand, will surely take into account the penalty he is liable to suffer if he is caught.

It isn't easy to say how far the death-penalty actually operates as a deterrent, either in the first or in the second degree, or to estimate how much difference, if it does deter, its abolition would make in the murder-rate. Some European countries abolished it many years ago, and some of them have re-introduced it. There are voluminous statistics recording the murder rate in all, or almost all, those countries before and after abolition, and these statistics are appealed to in support of their case both by those who oppose the death-penalty and by those who defend it. A confusing factor is that many countries abandoned the death-penalty in practice, and began automatically to reprieve all, or almost all, convicted murderers, many years before they abolished it formally: this casts doubt on the significance of the statistics, and of the graphs extrapolated from the statistics, which seem to indicated that abolition made no difference to the rate; in those countries the actual abolition was a 'non-event.'

The opponents of the death-penalty make the main plank in their case the contention that it is not a uniquely efficient deterrent—if, indeed, it deters at all—and that prolonged imprisonment would be just as efficacious. They have other practical arguments besides: it is irrevocable, and you may have made a mistake; and if you execute an innocent man, you can't bring him back to life—to which supporters of capital punishment reply that the law is hedged about with such safeguards, at any rate in England, that the execution of an innocent man is not a practical possibility.

Other arguments—still less cogent, in my opinion—are put forward: the process of carrying out an execution, it is said, brutalizes the members of the prison staff who have to take part in it, and has a deplorable psychological effect on the other inmates of the prison where it takes place.

As I have said, I don't want to evaluate the arguments on one side and the other, or to attempt to decide between them, because I think that all this arguing, as far as the opponents of capital punishment are concerned, is simply shadow-boxing. What really counts with them, or most of them, is not reason or argument, but a deep feeling of revulsion from the whole thing—a humanitarian feeling, the feeling that, in a civilized country in the twentieth century, the State can't kill a man in cold blood. Forget all the arguments based on the brutalization of the prison staff or the possibility that an innocent man may be executed; forget deterrence; assume, if you like, that you will deter twenty murderers by electrocuting or guillotining or hanging one guilty murderer—you just can't do it; it is simply barbaric, and there's an end to it.

Ah, but—the defenders of capital punishment will reply—an execution today isn't the barbarous affair that it was in the bad old days, not much more than a hundred years ago, when men were hanged in public, and crowds gathered outside the prison to enjoy the spectacle, and drink flowed freely, and a cheer was raised when the executioner pulled the bolt that launched the prisoner into eternity. It is all very different now: it all takes place in privacy, and the whole thing is conducted with decorum and dispatch.

That is quite true. Today an execution is a very scientific, very clinical affair. Let me read you a description from a little book, *A Life for a Life?* written by Sir Ernest Gowers, a civil servant who was Chairman of the Royal Commission from whose report I have quoted. Here is Sir Ernest Gowers' account of what happens (or what used to happen) at an execution in Britain in modern, up-to-date, conditions: 'The Under-Sheriff, to whom the High Sheriff usually assigns this part of his duties, arrives at the prison about twenty minutes before the time of the execution—it is always 8 o'clock in the morning. A few minutes before eight he goes with the Governor and the Medical Officer to the execution chamber. The executioner and his assistant will be then be waiting outside the door of the condemned cell, together with the Chief Officer and the officer detailed to conduct the prisoner to the gallows. The Under-Sheriff gives a signal, and the executioner and the officers enter the cell. The executioner pinions the prisoner's arms behind his back. He is then escorted to the execution chamber, with one officer on each side and the Chaplain preceding. The Under-Sheriff, Governor and Medical Officer enter the chamber by another door.

'The prisoner is placed on the trap on a spot marked in white chalk, in such a position that his feet are directly across the division of the doors. The executioner draws a white cap over his head and places the noose round his neck; the assistant executioner pinions his legs. As soon as the executioner sees that all is ready, he goes to the lever and pulls it. It is all done very quickly. The time between the entry of the executioner into the condemned cell and the pulling of the lever is normally about ten seconds; in a few prisons, where the execution chamber does not adjoin the condemned cell, it may be longer, but seldom more than twenty-five seconds.' What, you may

211

ask, could be more civilized or more expeditious than that?

Yes: I know it is all conducted in the most civilized fashion, but does that make it any the more acceptable to the humanitarian? In a way it makes it more ghastly.

Perhaps I might here tell a story of a personal experience, the nearest I ever got to attending an execution myself. It was more than twenty years ago; I was visiting an old college friend of mine who lived in the County of Norfolk. He lived alone with his mother, in a beautiful old house, the ancestral home of his family, not luxuriously but in great comfort. He was a scholarly person, who edited eighteenth-century authors and wrote articles on local history in archaeological magazines; gentle, kind, considerate; the sort of man who wouldn't hurt a fly. He met me at the railway station at Norwich in his very comfortable car. I hadn't seen him for some time, and as we drove through the quiet Norfolk countryside I asked him what news he had of himself. He said he had recently been appointed Under-Sheriff of the County of Norfolk, a post which involved him from time to time in formal ceremonial duties. The Queen had visited Norwich not long before, and he had had to be in attendance. 'It all went off very well,' said my friend. It occurred to me to ask whether it wouldn't fall to him as Under-Sheriff to be in attendance at executions, if any prisoners were condemned to death at the Norwich Assizes; I said that I hoped he hadn't had to undergo that experience—I thought (though I didn't say so) that he simply wouldn't have been able to face it. My friend said that when he accepted the post of Under-Sheriff, the Sheriff had offered to appoint a deputy to attend at the prison if by any chance an execution should take place during his term of office. 'But,' said my friend, 'I declined the appointment of a deputy. I felt that, if the occasion arose, it was my duty to go through with it. It would be a valuable experience.' 'Well,' I said, 'I hope it won't fall to your lot.' 'As a matter of fact,' he replied, 'there was an execution in Norwich last week,' and he explained that it had been a double execution: two young men had been condemned to death at the Assizes; each, in a fit of passion, had murdered his girl; and it was thought fitting that they should be hanged together. They consented, and so it took place; 'I think they really preferred it that way,' said my friend. 'But were you actually in the execution chamber?' I asked. 'Of course,' he answered. 'I suppose it's a big room,' I said, hopefully, 'and you were at the far end of it?' 'Oh, no,' he replied, 'it's a very small room; I wasn't more than a few feet away.' I didn't know what to say; there was a pause. 'It all went off very well,' said

213

my friend, 'I was home in time for breakfast. . . . Ah, here we are'—and he brought the car to a halt in front of his ancestral mansion, where his old mother was waiting for him on the steps. My friend, I repeat, was a very humane man. But it occurred to me that he was also a very tough man, tougher than I had supposed. I looked at him with admiration, an admiration not unmixed with horror. Horror—why?

Well, let me quote some verses by Ralph Hodgson, an English poet who migrated to the United States towards the end of his life, and died in Ohio ten years or so ago:

> To hang a man:
> To fit the cap,
> And fix the rope,
> And slide the bar,
> And let him drop.
> I know, I know:
> What can you do!
> You have no choice,
> You're driven to;
> You can't be soft—
> A man like that;
> But Oh it seems—
> I don't know what—
> To hang a man!

Well, you can't argue against that: it is a matter of feeling. Statistics about the deterrent effect of the death-penalty, even if conclusive in its favour, are irrelevant—you just can't hang a man in England today: that is what the opponents of capital punishment, I believe—or nine out of ten of them—are saying. Suppose you could prove that by executing, and only by executing, half-a-dozen murderers a year you would save the lives of half-a-dozen, or a dozen, or a score, or even a hundred innocent victims—night-watchmen, bank guards, policemen, prison warders, or old ladies murdered so that the murderer could steal their savings—you still shouldn't do it. Better that a hundred innocent human beings should be murdered than that half-a-dozen guilty murderers should be executed. That is the attitude of the humanitarians.

Do you agree with them? I do not. But I have to confess that if it could be proved that torture—the thumbscrew, the rack, boiling oil, or a more painful method of putting people to death, say burning them alive—would increase the deterrent effect of the death-penalty, and save a few more innocent lives every year, I don't think I could bring myself to support a law introducing such punishments. And my reason, if it is a reason, for taking up that position is just the same as the humanitarian's reason, if it is a reason, for opposing capital punishment: torturing people in cold blood is something you can't do in a civilized country today.

Let me now turn from the criminal law to the field of education. I don't mean university education: in a university the problem of discipline—what you do to people if they break the rules—only arises in exceptional circumstances: there are so few rules to break. I mean education in schools; and the schools I want to draw your special attention to, because they provide the most striking illustration of the point I want to make, are those private schools in Great Britain—misleadingly called 'Public Schools'—where the sons of what used to be called the upper classes, and of the middle classes, are educated between the ages of twelve and eighteen. They are most of them ancient foundations; some of them date back to the days before the Reformation; some of them were founded during the succeeding centuries; all of them are independent of control by the State.

Side by side with the Public Schools there are the State Schools, set up during the last hundred years under a series of Education Acts, which are financed and controlled by the State and provide a compulsory education for children whose parents can't afford, or don't wish, to send them to private schools.

How do State Schools and Public Schools in Britain deal with the problem of enforcing discipline? To appreciate the answer to this question, one must look at the different conditions under

216

which the two kinds of school carry out their task.

The State School is a building comprising class-rooms with an adjoining playground, where children go every morning to be taught, returning to their families when afternoon school is over. Enforcing discipline in such a school means little more than keeping order in class; it is effected by a teacher, by means of personality, reinforced on occasions, not very menacingly, and not very frequently, I suspect, by a cane: 'Hold out your hand!' in the presence of the class—that sort of thing.

For the Public School, discipline presents a very different problem, at once more complex and more difficult. To understand the difference, you must bear in mind that the Public Schools are boarding schools, in which boys and masters—I say 'boys and masters' because the Public Schools are, by and large, all-male establishments—live together, day in, day out, in a little self-contained world, governed by customs and traditions which vary from one school to another, but have a common stamp—'the Public School stamp'—which they imprint on the pupils who pass through them. The phrase 'a Public School man' has, or used to have, a definite social, not to say snobbish, implication. The Public Schools, until Victorian days, were a sort of playground for the children of the gentry and the aristocracy. Then

217

came Dr Arnold, the father of Matthew Arnold, who was Headmaster of Rugby School in the 1830s, and who will be familiar to any one who has read *Tom Brown's School Days* or Lytton Strachey's *Eminent Victorians*. Largely as a result of the influence of Dr Arnold and the model that he created at Rugby, the Public Schools became the training ground of the British governing class, so long as we had a governing class, and educated the civil servants who ran the British Empire, so long as there was a British Empire.

The backbone of the Public School system was—and still is—the prefectorial system. The masters, of course, do the teaching and make the rules, and ultimate power resides with them; the prefects are senior boys to whom the master delegates a measure of his authority. This teaches them how to wield power responsibly, and is (or is supposed to be) an important part of their education.

Together with the prefectorial system goes the system of 'fagging.' The prefects are served and waited upon by 'fags,' junior boys, usually in their first year, who have to perform menial tasks for their seniors, the prefects—running errands for them, cleaning their shoes, dusting their books, making tea and washing up, fetching and carrying, calling them in the morning, and so on. To keep the fags in order, and to ensure that they carry out their duties efficiently, the prefects can inflict punishments, and the commonest and most effective form of punishment—anyhow until recently—was beating. The instrument employed was regularly a cane; in my old school it was an ashplant, called a ground ash. Really serious offences would be dealt with by the housemaster, and a housemaster's beating was a solemn affair—less painful, perhaps, than a prefect's beating (the prefects were often chosen for strength and athletic ability) but a more impressive occasion; a prefect's beating was an everyday occurrence. (I don't mean that someone was beaten every day, but simply that it was a by no means rare event). It was a convenient and acceptable form of punishment, expeditious, humiliating, exemplary—and often preferred by the victim to such alternatives as tedious periods of detention, a troublesome imposition, or a suspension of privileges.

Of course this system depended, if it was to work fairly and well, upon the character and morale of the prefects, and upon adequate supervision by the housemaster. In a good house, all went well. But the system gave plenty of scope, in a bad house, to a prefect who was a bully or a sadist. From time to time there were exposures of abuses of their power on the part of the prefects: you can read about the kind of thing that happened in novels of school life and autobiographies of sensitive men whose personalities were scarred and marred—or who believe that their personalities were scarred and marred—by the brutalities and the injustices—or what seemed to them the brutalities and the injustices—that they had undergone at the hands of their seniors in their schooldays. But, on the whole, the system worked well. Most old Public School men, or at least most Public School men of the older generations, will tell you 'I was beaten pretty often when I was at Rugby (or Charterhouse, or Harrow, or wherever it was they went to), and it never did me any harm.' 'In fact' they will often go on to say, 'it did me all the good in the world'. Personally, if I were cross-examined about my own school experience, I should have to admit that I belong to this latter class: I was beaten pretty often, and I don't believe a beating ever did me any harm.

Having said so much, perhaps I owe it to myself to add that, when I became a prefect, I never beat anyone at all. This was not due to conscientious scruples on my part. I shouldn't have enjoyed beating anyone, and I managed to get on without doing it.

What is the attitude towards corporal punishment adopted today in the Public Schools? To judge from what is happening in my own old school—and from what I hear about other Public

Schools—the prefectorial system, the exercise of authority by senior over junior boys, is being eroded, and in particular—and this is the point I want to bring home—the 'prefect's beating' is practically a thing of the past. It is on its way out, if it isn't actually extinct. And why? Not because the victims have risen in rebellion on the grounds of justice or egalitarian feeling, not because the small boys refuse to allow themselves to be beaten, but because the prefects decline to beat them: the practice has gone out, it is out of fashion, it is contrary to the humanitarian tendency of the day.

It is out of fashion, not only with the prefects, but with the masters also. 'It hurts me more than it hurts you,' old-fashioned parents or school-masters used to say, as they applied the birch-rod to the tender bodies of their unfortunate offspring or pupils. If the remark was quoted against them, as it often was, that was because it was thought to be insincere: if they didn't actually enjoy beating their children, at least—or so it was thought—it gave them satisfaction to administer what they believed to be a healthy discipline.

So it was in the old days. Today, 'enlightened' parents and schoolmasters, at least in Britain, rarely chastise children: to do so really would hurt them more than it would hurt the victims. But—I can't help asking—if that is their reason for re-fraining from enforcing discipline, are they not

221

really being self-indulgent at the expense of those committed to their charge? 'Spare the rod, and spoil the child,' said the old adage. I don't know whether it contains a truth; I wouldn't confidently assert that corporal punishment is a necessary feature of scholastic discipline, any more than I would assert that it is necessary to retain capital punishment in order to protect society from the murderer. But I do suggest that, if such punishments, whether in the world of school or in the wider sphere of law-enforcement, are indeed a necessary means, or even the most effective means, of maintaining order, then the authorities are betraying their trust if they refrain from imposing them simply because they cannot bear to contemplate the infliction of pain and suffering that their imposition would involve. They ought not to spare the rod simply in order to spare themselves.

Perhaps I have dwelt too long on capital and corporal punishment. They are the issues in regard to which the humanitarian tendency that I am concerned with shows itself most obviously. But that tendency is at work also, I think, on a wider front. It isn't merely the infliction of pain or suffering that is in question: it is the imposition of authority by force. There is observable today a strong anti-authoritarian tendency, a tendency that makes itself felt, especially, but not exclusively, among the younger generation. I don't think that it offers a real threat to society, at any rate in Britain. Most people, after all, accept the fact that the running of the country, the continuance of civil society, depends in the end upon force, and are prepared themselves to appeal to force in order to maintain it: if occasion arises, they will call the police. But there certainly is in Britain, as I imagine there is in the United States, an increasing number of people who won't go along with that at all. They are hostile to the concept of authority, and they regard the police as their natural enemies. Of course, the considerations that sway them are mixed, and often muddled. Some of them simply won't accept the fact that force should play a part in human affairs, in human relationships: that is the pure humanitarian attitude. Others resent the fact that force should be used in order to maintain a society that they disapprove of—a society that they disapprove of on egalitarian and libertarian grounds. That is a sort of political humanitarianism.

I said that I supposed that this anti-authoritarian attitude was observable in the United States. Since I first drafted this paper, I came upon an article that offers, in an entirely different context, some confirmation of this view. The editor of a magazine called *The Washington*

Monthly, Mr Tom Bethell, in reviewing some of the latest contributions to the literature concerning the Kennedy assassination, asks how it is that so many wild and monstrous theories of conspiracy are put forward, seeking to implicate in the assassination members of the Government, members of the Supreme Court, even the White House itself. 'Why has this tendency become so noticeable recently?' asks Mr Bethell. 'At first, superficially, it may appear to be nothing more than a desire to avoid seeming naive, but there is more to it than this. It is more than a fear of seeming naive, there is an actual hostility, a burning rage, a desire to take the offensive against the *status quo* no matter what. Even a willingness, if necessary, to chop off the branch one is resting on. One is finally forced to the conclusion that there are in any society a good many individuals who naturally have or mysteriously develop a strong anti-authoritarian bias, a bias against any order, any institution, any stability, any society.'

There are in Britain, as in the United States, an increasing number of people who are hostile to authority; with us, they are a comparatively new phenomenon, and there aren't very many of them. Who are they? Where do they come from? What do they represent? What is it that they complain about? What is it that they want?

They would not claim to represent the oppressed and downtrodden, the underpaid and overworked, the poor, the lower classes. They come themselves, most of them, from bourgeois homes, and are inclined to be ashamed of the fact. They don't want to rebel, to organize revolt or revolution, to take over power from its present holders (though they are often duped and exploited by political manipulators of the extreme Left who wish to do exactly that). They are repelled by society as it is organized today, and feel that they have no place in it; it is dehumanized, dominated by money and machines, a world of pylons and nylons, of computers and commuters, ruled by forces, whether of the Right or the Left, over which the individual has no control—the individual, who is so occupied with the business of making a living that he is unable to live his own life. 'Make love, not war!' is one of their messages to the world; 'Make love, not money!' should surely be another.

People who recoil from the horrors of contemporary civilization—and I would be the last to deny the reality of those horrors—and who no longer accept traditional religious beliefs and the conventional code of morals, are all too likely to succumb to the appeal of a humanitarian gospel—Christianity without dogma or discipline: resist the police by offering them flowers, the emblem of love; overcome evil with good; love your enemies; love everyone, with an amorphous, all-embracing love—the sort of religion that inspires a community of hippies. In the words of a contemporary evangelist, 'They bring the oldest message of love and peace and laughter, and trust in God and don't worry, trust in the future and don't fight; and trust in your kids, and don't worry because it's all beautiful and right.'

I am against the hippies' ideal for two reasons. First because I think that their muddled mysticism, their refusal to think and to be guided by reason, makes them an easy prey, not only to crackpots like Dr Timothy Leary, from whom I have just been quoting, but to more mischievous rabble-rousers like Professor Herbert Marcuse, who seek to upset the foundations of society. Marcuse calls upon his young nonconformist followers to effect what he describes as 'methodical desublimation of traditional culture by means of counter-violence, direct action, and uncivil disobedience in every sphere of life.' This social sabotage is to be directed against the beautiful in the established culture, against its all too sublimated, segregated, orderly, harmonizing forms. So he is all in favour of anti-art (pending the complete abolition of art by its absorption into life), together with black music and 'its avant-gardistic white equivalent,' and he approves of drug-taking (the trip, he says, involves the dissolution of the ego shaped by the established society) and of the atmosphere in which, as he puts it, 'the hatred of the young bursts into laughter and song, mixing the barricade and the dance floor, love play and heroism [*heroism* is the reading of the Penguin text: I suspect a misprint for *heroin*].' He recommends the methodical use of obscenities, as practised by black and white radicals, in order to effect 'a methodical subversion of the linguistic universe of the establishment'; President X and Governor Y he says, should be called Pig X and Pig Y, and addressed as motherfuckers, because they are men who have perpetrated the unspeakable Oedipal crime. He approves not only of dirty language, but of dirty bodies, welcoming 'the erotic belligerency in the songs of protest, the sensuousness of long hair, of the body unsoiled by plastic cleanliness.'

That is humanitarianism gone wrong: violence called upon in aid of, in the name of, nonviolence, with the promise of perpetual revolution.

There is a danger that those who are disenchanted with society as it is, and who have renounced the guidance of traditional wisdom, may fall victims to such desperate and dangerous nonsense.

My second reason for opposing the ideal lived out in a community of hippies—loving everyone,

227

hating no one, harming no one, just co-existing peaceably—is that I think that this ideal, even if it could be achieved for society as a whole without revolution, is an evil one, and one that involves the sacrifice of everything that makes life worth living, everything that raises man above the level of domesticated animals.

The humanitarian ideal has, I know—in England at least—a special appeal to the young: I described earlier the life-style of the Oxford student—or of a large proportion of Oxford students—which is evidently inspired by a desire to return to nature, to recover the primitive innocence of man: the shaggy heads, the grotesque whiskers, the pathetic beards, the bare feet, the walking hand in hand, the patched clothes, the scruffiness, the dirt—all these are symbolic: they are the outward signs of a deep-seated desire to escape from the world as it is today into a primaeval paradise. I don't think—I hope I'm not being too optimistic—that there is any likelihood of an increase in the hippy population in Great Britain, still less of their ideal winning general acceptance, though it is certainly not without influence on educated opinion. Most of the young in Britain learn to come to terms with the world in which they live, to make the best of it. Most of them, when they go down from the university, cut their hair, put on decent clothes, apply for jobs, and settle down to earn their livings: they enter the world instead of dropping out of it. Far be it from me to adopt a superior or patronizing attitude towards them, to say to them, when they join the ranks of the conformists, 'I told you so.' What I do want to say to them is that they should not regret the loss of their humanitarian ideals, and that they needn't feel ashamed of their apostasy.

Humanity, humaneness, is a good thing: it distinguishes men from animals, and civilized men from savages; but it is a good thing of which it is possible to have too much. Refusal ever to impose force on others would mean the dissolution of civilized society. So long as there are bad men about, society relies ultimately upon force to restrain them: civilization depends upon the use of force just as much as it depends upon eliminating the abuse of force—indeed, it relies upon a proper use of force to protect its members from the wrongful use of force. You may recall the story of the shipwrecked sailors, who after tossing about for many days and nights in an open boat on uncharted seas, caught sight at last of an island. As dawn came on and they scanned the coast they were approaching, they perceived something— was it a tree?—standing upon the horizon. As they drew near, they made out what is was: a gibbet, with a dead body hanging from it. 'Thank

God!', exclaimed one of them, 'it's a civilized country!' Well, I know what he had in mind: in a country where you may be executed by the hangman, at least you aren't likely to be scalped by savages or eaten by cannibals.

If a society refuses to contemplate the deliberate infliction of suffering upon its members, or by some of its members upon others, then it is at the mercy of its enemies, external or internal. The subsistence of law and order is the first essential of civilization.

Suppose a society from which, by a miracle, all wrong-thinking people were excluded, a community of gentle human beings, ruled by universal benevolence. Surely such a world would be the dreariest of deserts—no strife, yes, and no hate: but no excellence, no culture, no genius, no art, and no passionate love.

In the actual world, no extreme of excellence or virtue in human beings is conceivable without at least the possibility of its opposite—no passionate love without the possibility of hate, no ecstasy of pleasure without the possibility of pain. It is only in heaven that that condition will be transcended. Meanwhile, a wise man will make the best he can of this imperfect world. In a welter of good and evil, he will lead a measured life, compromising, yielding, standing firm, fighting if need be, keeping a clear head well screwed on, and a warm
230

heart in the right place. In their eagerness to eliminate the evil, the humanitarians are ready to forgo the good; and their longing—did they but know it—is for the dead level of an impossible Utopia, devoid of pain, passion, and nobility.

A Utopia, indeed: but we need not look far to see something like such a community in action— or in passivity. In the aftermath of a pop festival, when the influence of the hysterical music has abated, or at a love-in, where the air is sweet with cannabis, one may observe the passionless population of a Woodstock world anticipating that Utopian bliss: tender human creatures, tame and same, with the tameness and sameness of a herd of deer, or a school of porpoises, or a gathering of Galapagos lizards—a huddle of bodies snuggling, not struggling, on the smooth firm sand and gently respiring under the warm rays of the broad bland sun.

Liberty

I suppose that almost everybody in Great Britain today, and almost everybody in the United States,

231

if challenged on the subject of free speech, would say that he was in favour of it—though he might not be clear in his mind about what he meant by 'free' or about what was to be included in the notion of 'speech.' Does 'speech' in this context extend, for example, to printed and published words? Does it cover not only verbal but also pictorial and other forms of self-expression? Does it include every form of verbal utterance? In the course of arguments about free speech, extreme libertarians sometimes invoke the saying attributed to Voltaire: 'I detest what you say; I will defend to the death your right to say it,' as if Voltaire were asserting that everyone ought always to be allowed to say whatever he liked. But what the great freethinker was really contending for was (surely?) no more than the right to the uninhibited expression of opinion, the freedom of trade in ideas; he wasn't thinking about foul language, or obscenities. And it is the free expression of opinion that most people, I think, are concerned about when they say they are in favour of free speech.

In the United States freedom of speech is positively guaranteed by the constitution. Just what that freedom comprises has been laid down in a number of enactments and judicial decisions that constitute a whole branch of the law; and the same, making allowance for the fact that the

English have no written constitution, is true in Great Britain. I am not concerned here with what the law actually is, either in Britain or in the United States. I am going to ask what the law ought to be, in regard to one particular area of human life or human conduct: how far ought the law to allow people freedom not merely to exress opinions, but to express themselves? I think I detect, in society today, a strong feeling that human beings ought to be guaranteed by law not merely the right to express their opinions freely, but the right to express themselves as they choose, whether as creative artists or writers or in their everyday relations with each other. I should like to suggest that there is a danger that that claim may be pushed too far. Freedom to express one's self is a good thing, but it is a good thing that one can have too much of.

Most of the people who say simply that they are in favour of free speech would probably agree that there must be some limitations upon the freedom they contend for. For instance, everyone, except a professed anarchist, would surely agree that limitations may—indeed, should—be imposed by the civil law upon each citizen's right of free speech in order to protect the private right of other citizens: the law of slander, the law of libel, and the law of copyright, all of them restrict —and, most people would say, very properly

233

restrict—in the interests of other individuals, the fundamental right of every individual to say or print whatever he pleases. Restrictions upon this right are also imposed, in the interests of the public at large, by the criminal law. The law, at least the law of Britain, and I suspect the same is true in the United States, makes it a criminal offence to utter or to publish words likely to create a breach of the peace; and in the field of security, the law makes it a criminal offence to publish in time of peace official secrets or seditious matter, and in time of war information that is likely to be of assistance to the enemy.

A recent example of encroachment by the criminal law in Britain upon this fundamental freedom is the Race Relations Act passed in 1965. This Act made it an offence to publish or distribute, with intent to stir up hatred against certain sections of the public specified in the Act, written matter which is insulting and likely to stir up such hatred. To constitute an offence it is not necessary, as it is under the Public Order Act, that the publication or distribution should be in a public place, or that it should be likely to cause a breach of the peace.

Most people would agree that all these restrictions upon the fundamental right to speak freely are justifiable on the ground that they help to preserve an orderly and civilized society; and until recently, I think, most people agreed that the law should aim also at preserving public decency, and that, with that end in view, it might impose restrictions not only on behaviour, but also on speech and writing: if the law could properly forbid people to do in public things which offend other people's sense of decency, why shouldn't it forbid people publicly to say things—or exhibit things in writing, or for that matter in pictures—that give similar offence? In other words, it was generally accepted that the fundamental right of free speech and free expression is a right that is subject to the requirements of public decency just as it is subject to the requirements of public safety and public order.

This generally accepted position is now under attack from several quarters, both as regards speech and as regards other forms of self-expression. On what do the critics or attackers base their attack? To what arguments or principles do they appeal? There are, I think, three main grounds of objection.

First, the critics say that the concepts of obscenity and indecency are not constant, that they vary from place to place and age to age. What is considered indecent or obscene in one part of the world is perfectly acceptable in another; things that shocked our grandfathers, or even our fathers, seem quite innocuous to us today. To legislate against the obscene is like trying to legislate against a chameleon by reference to its colour.

Further, say the critics, the concepts obscenity and indecency vary not only from one age and one place to another; there is rarely, if ever, agreement about them even in the same place and time; certainly there is not agreement in Great Britain today about what is obscene or indecent and what is not. Since the concepts are so uncertain in their denotation, it is impossible to frame a satisfactory law to deal with them; for it is a fundamental juridical principle that all laws, especially those to which a criminal sanction is attached, should state clearly and precisely what it is that they forbid.

Finally, the critics' third objection is that it isn't merely that no two people agree—or at any rate most people disagree—about the application of these concepts; the fact is (they say) that no one, no single person, can say what he himself means by them. When a man says 'That's indecent,' or 'That's obscene,' he is not indicating an attribute of the thing he refers to, but simply expressing his own reaction to it. To legislate against obscenity, therefore, is not only to legislate against a chameleon, it is to legislate against a chimera, a subjective fantasy.

To each of these three objections I think a satisfactory answer can be given.

The answer to the first objection is very simple.

It is perfectly true that the things or the conduct thought or felt to be indecent or obscene differ widely in different countries, different societies, different civilizations, and they very also from one age, one generation even, to another. But, after all, each society legislates only for itself, and not for other societies, and only for its contemporaries and not for past or future generations. Therefore, provided the law takes account of the opinions and feelings prevailing in the community, and is so drafted that it can be adapted as those feelings and opinions change, it does not seem relevant to observe that it would have been inappropriate, or even absurd, to have passed such a law in a society where different feelings prevailed.

That is, I think, an obvious and sufficient answer; but one shouldn't dismiss this objector out of hand—his objection may conceal a deeper and more serious criticism. 'I will tell you,' he may really be saying, 'why the notions of indecency and obscenity are so variable. It is because they are not founded upon reason, they are elements in a structure of conventions built out of, and upon, irrational taboos. Social progress consists in discarding taboos in favour of a rational structure of social rules; any law that bolsters up such conventions is an obstacle to progress.' I think this criticism is ill-founded. I would question the

237

premise that progress consists in, or depends upon, the discarding of non-rational conventions and taboos; and here, I suspect, I would have the support of social anthropologists, who would surely tell us that civilization is a highly artificial construction, and that to maintain it we must observe conventions which are in part rational and in part non-rational, and that it is impossible, and would be harmful even if it were not impossible, to eliminate the non-rational elements from the complex web of existing social convention. A society of human beings whose actions are governed entirely by rational considerations is hardly a conceivable, let alone an attainable, ideal. Indeed, it is not even a desirable ideal, for it is not true that the nearer we come to achieving it, the better life will be. We ought rather to aim at an appropriate blending of the non-rational and the rational: progress consists in the refinement, not in the elimination, of taboos; society, in short, should have the courage of its conventions.

So much for the objection based upon variability and irrationality.

The second objector is more practical in his outlook that the first. 'Never mind,' he says, 'about other countries and other times; forget all *a priori* objections, based on irrationality and the like; let us assume that we want to legislate against obscenity in this country today. Very well:

but how can we frame a satisfactory law? Even if we agree about the concepts of indecency and obscenity in the abstract, there is no agreement, when you come to apply them in practice, about what the things are that they denote: the concepts turn out to be hopelessly vague and ragged at the edges. The writer, the artist, the publisher, the man in the street, all of them, if they are to be made liable to criminal prosecution, are entitled to be told in clear, precise, and definite terms what it is that they may not write or publish or say or do. It is impossible to frame a law against indecency that satisfies this requirement.'

'Clear, precise, and definite terms'—the requirement may seem very reasonable, but it is not quite as simple as it sounds. Clarity, precision, and definiteness are no doubt aims that every legislator sets himself, but it is not always possible for him to achieve them. Clarity is one thing, precision and definiteness (which we may call synonymous, I think, in this context) are another. Sometimes in a law both are attainable; sometimes precision but not clarity; sometimes clarity but not precision—it all depends upon the subject matter of the legislation. The liability imposed by taxation, for instance, is always precise and definite, but the meaning of the law imposing it, as anyone will know who has had to deal with his own income tax, is not always clear; it is often

239

exceedingly—and inevitably—obscure, because the cases that a taxing statute has to deal with are so intricate that they can only be provided for in very complicated and difficult terms. On the other hand, there are large ares in which, owing to the nature of the subject matter, the legislature cannot make rules as exact and precise as those that impose our tax liabilities; it has to forgo definiteness and to lay down a rule couched in clear but general terms, leaving it to a jury (with a judge's guidance) to determine whether in the circumstances of the particular case the defendant's conduct did or did not transgress the rule laid down.

Take the British Road Traffic Acts. They, or regulations made under them, lay down precisely the speed limit to be observed on certain roads and in certain areas; it is a question of fact, the answer to which is ascertainable by reference to a stop-watch, whether or not at any moment a driver is exceeding the relevant limit. He always knows, therefore, or can find out by looking at his speedometer, whether he is breaking the law or not. True enough: but motorists often, without exceeding the speed limit, drive recklessly or dangerously. Obviously, it is impossible to define recklessness in a statute, or to lay down precisely what shall constitute dangerous driving. The law does not on that account abandon the attempt to legislate against such driving; it simply prohibits dangerous driving, undefined, and leaves it to the jury in each case to say, in the light of the evidence, whether the defendant did or did not drive dangerously.

So, too, with cruelty to children: cruelty cannot be defined in a statute so precisely that a man can say to himself 'The Cruelty to Children Act is clear, precise, and definite: I can hit my child so many blows, of so much force, without transgressing the law; it is only if I exceed the cruelty limit cleary and precisely laid down by Parliament, that I shall be guilty.' The legislature does not therefore say—and no one would wish it to say—'Since cruelty cannot be precisely defined, we will not prohibit it, but will leave it to the good feeling and self-restraint of the public, and of parents in particular, to see to it that children are not subject to cruel treatment.' No: the law prohibits cruelty, and leaves it to a jury of ordinary men and women to say whether in the given case the defendant's conduct is to be considered cruel.

In order to reach a verdict in such cases, a juryman must not have regard to what he himself would tolerate or disapprove, he must not ask himself what he would have done in the circumstances; he must put aside any peculiarities or prejudices of his own and decide, as best he can, what a reasonable person would do, or would tolerate, or would disapprove, in such a case. No doubt it is often difficult to ascertain this standard; and no doubt it is more often difficult to do so when you are dealing with indecency than it is in other areas—the borderline cases may be more numerous, partly because the borderline is in that area a shifting one—but the task that confronts the jury is essentially the same. It is important to insist on this, because the critics of anti-indecency legislation often suggest that it imposes on juries an impossible task, and one that they do not have to carry out in cases arising out of legislation in other fields.

The fact, then, is that obscenity and indecency, like cruelty, negligence, and recklessness, are concepts that do not lend themselves to precise definition; but it does not follow from this that we should abandon the attempt to legislate against them.

The case presented by the third objector is the most plausible of the three, but it is no better founded than that of the other two. This objector does not concern himself with taboos and conventions, or with the fact that people often disagree about what is indecent and what is not; he takes a slightly different stand: 'What you are complaining about,' he says, 'is nothing more than a personal reaction, and one which you cannot justify or even explain. You say you are shocked. What do you mean by "shocked"? Weren't you shocked by newspaper reports of what went on in Vietnam? You say you are disgusted. Aren't you disgusted by what you read about the conditions in which the poor are housed in London slums? You complain about obscenities in the field of sex: is anything in the whole field of sex as obscene as apartheid in South Africa? You do not press for legislation against reports containing accounts of shocking, disgusting, obscenities like these. Even in the field of sex you betray the same inconsistency. A picture shocks you more than a verbal description of the thing depicted. You are not shocked by the idea of copulation in the marriage bed, but you are shocked by the idea of copulation in the street. What exactly is it that you are shocked by, and why is it that you are shocked by it? Perhaps it would do you good,' he might add, with a touch of self-righteous asperity, 'to be exposed to being shocked a bit more often, and then you might stop being shocked by things that in themselves are perfectly innocuous.'

To this the complainant might well modestly reply: 'Of course I know that all these words—"shocking" and "horrifying," "disgusting" and "obscene"—are sometimes applied to things quite different from the things I am complaining about. We may say, no doubt, that we are horrified by the news of a railway accident involving heavy loss of life, and that we are shocked when we hear that the Bishop has been murdered on the steps of the Cathedral; we are disgusted by the Government's measures to deal with unemployment, and if we want to convey to a friend our impression of the unpardonable ugliness of a third party, we may, perhaps, apply the word "obscene" to his or her appearance. The feelings that I am talking about,' he might go on to say, 'which are experienced by most people with any refinement of sensibility, are quite different from the feelings at work in those examples. I cannot give you a clear and rational account of these feelings of mine, or enumerate the things that evoke them; they differ from indignation and moral disapproval, though they are sometimes accompanied by those emotions. My horror and disgust at actually witnessing an act of physical cruelty, for instance, are distinct from my pity for the victim and my moral disapproval of the act. Shame and disgust are usually evoked by functions of the body—for example, sexual intercourse, excretion, and parturition. These processes seem to be usually associated somehow with shame—the shame that craves privacy, the shame that Adam and Eve felt when they knew that they were naked. These feelings of shame and disgust are evoked—I don't know why— more easily by seeing something than by reading about it, unless the description is visually vivid.

244

They are complex: the emotion felt is often accompanied by a physical reaction—a revulsion stronger than distaste and amounting sometimes to nausea. I know,' he might conclude, 'that these feelings—which I share, you must remember, with many people of normal sensibility, who are upset in the same way and by the same kinds of thing as I am myself—are not rational, and I know that they are difficult, perhaps just because they are not rational, to account for and to classify. But that does not make them any the less genuine, or any the less disagreeable, or any the less deserving—surely?—of the attention of the law.'

That seems to me a more than sufficient answer to the third objection. Let me support it by an illustration. Suppose that a man, in full view and hearing of persons passing by him in the street, exposes his private parts, proceeds, for good measure, to masturbate in public, and having masturbated, to utter a string of 'four-letter' words, and to display a poster with filthy words and pictures printed on it. Surely it is as reasonable that the law should protect the passers-by from the third kind of affront (the filthy posters) as from the second (the foul language), and from the second as from the first (the indecent exposure), and surely it is as reasonable that it should protect passers-by from any one of these things as it is that it should protect them from actual physical

245

assault? A law that in such a context protects the citizen's person but not his susceptibilities is like a divorce law that recognizes physical but not mental cruelty. And the fact that the complainant, where it is his susceptibilities that are assaulted, cannot define the kind of things that distress him, or explain why it is that they distress him as they do, affords no reason why the law should not protect him, so far as it can, from being subjected to the distress.

I should therefore look with favour on the idea of passing a law the aim of which was to protect the sensibilities of ordinary people from being outraged by the impact of things generally felt by them to be indecent. Of course, the law should not prudishly take account of mild or minor improprieties: whatever its wording, the test should be, in effect, whether the indecent act or thing complained of would be found outrageously offensive by a person of ordinary sensibility. It would be for the court, or jury, to decide in each case whether the limit had been exceeded.

I have spoken of protecting the public, and the examples I have given consisted of acts done in public places. Should the proposed prohibition apply only to things done or things exhibited in public? Many people who are in general opposed to censorship would, I believe, none the less approve of a law such as I have suggested, provided its scope was limited to acts publicly performed, or things publicly exhibited. And conversely, many people who strongly support a law forbidding indecency in public would hold that the line should be drawn there. If I may borrow the terminology of Roman law, they have no objection to the activities of the aedile, whose job it was to preserve decency on the streets; the man they object to is the censor, who claims jurisdiction over art and literature—books, pictures, the theatre, and films. They would not mind a law that protected the passer-by from having indecencies actually obtruded upon him in public, but further than that they would not go.

They would say, presumably, that it should not be an offence just to publish indecent writings or drawings (or books containing them), or to offer them, whether gratis or for sale, to individual members of the public or, indeed, to the public at large; in their view, you should be liable to prosecution only if you actually exhibit them, or the indecent elements in them, in a public place. The bookseller may offer such books for sale in his shop, but he must not display them, open at any indecent passage or illustration, in his window where they may catch the eye of the innocent passer-by. So too with indecent theatrical performances and indecent shows (of films, pictures, and the like); provided these don't take place

247

actually in public, no offence, they would say, should be deemed to have been committed, even if members of the public are allowed, or even invited, to view them, whether gratis or on payment of an entrance fee. In such cases, the argument would run, people can't complain that they have had indecency obtruded upon them; they needn't buy the book if it is offered for sale, or accept it if it is offered gratis; they needn't enter the premises where the performance is being given or the exhibition held. Once the aedile begins to turn the pages of a book, or crosses the threshold of premises that are private, he is exceeding his function as aedile and usurping the office of the censor.

I think that this contention takes too narrow a view of the legitimate functions of the aedile, and pushes too far the doctrine *caveat emptor* ('buyer's risk'); it fails to take account of the facts of life, of the way things actually happen. People when they buy a book don't always know, and can't be expected to know, what they will find inside it. Unless the law provides that a publisher must impress a special mark or label on all books likely to outrage generally accepted standards of decency, and draw attention to indecent passages in otherwise innocent books by a note on the cover or the title-page—'outrageous indecencies on pp. 7, 26, 141–42, 210–15'—people won't know when they buy a book whether they are going to find indecencies inside it. To say that people who buy a book or a ticket of admission to a theatre should have prepared themselves by reading what the critics in the weekly papers had to say about the book, and that if the critics have misled them about a play, they can always walk out of the theatre, is not a realistic answer to the problem. No more is it realistic to say to people, if they complain about being confronted by an obscenity on television, 'you can always switch the thing off.' After all, many people watch television together with the family, and it is no use telling them to switch it off themselves if half the family want to keep it on. And where books are concerned, it is not only the purchaser that has to be considered: once a book is bought, it is liable to fall into the hands of all and sundry—and the person who picks it up and begins to read it unsuspectingly is, to all intents and purposes, in the same position as the innocent passer-by who finds himself contronted by an obscene picture on a billboard.

On the whole, therefore, I should be in favour of a law prohibiting the presentation of indecencies—I mean, indecencies that could properly be classified as outrageous—not only in public places, but also in books and magazines, and in plays, films, and exhibitions to which the public has access. If it is reasonable that the law

249

should protect people from having thrust upon them, willy-nilly, things that outrage their sensibilities, it seems reasonable that it should likewise protect them from the risk of encountering such things at every turn in their daily life.

Some of the objections in principle that are advanced against legislation prohibiting indecency in books and plays and pictures are the same as those advanced against laws prohibiting indecency in public—the vagueness of the concept, the liability to change, the impossibility of defining it, and so on. I have already dealt with those objections; but there is a special objection that applies only to legislation in the field of art and literature, and to this I now turn.

The law, it is said, should not interfere in the field of books and plays and pictures, because Art should be above the law: it is monstrous, and it is absurd, to try to subject the creative activities of a painter or a writer, or an artist of any other kind, to the jurisdiction of a law court, giving to a judge or a jury the power of determining, when an artist's work is challenged, what subjects he may treat or depict and what language he may use in order to describe them. It would be equally monstrous, and even more absurd, to attempt to enforce decency by means of a list of prohibited subjects, words, and phrases, set out in a schedule to the relevant statute. Such absurdities, it is said, are the natural and inevitable result of transgressing the fundamental principle that the artist, working in his capacity as an artist, should not be subjected to the laws that regulate the activities of the ordinary citizen; the products of his creative gifts—in a word, Art—should be excluded from the scope of any law, or at least from the scope of any law intended to protect society from the impact of indecency. Of course, one can't help sympathizing with people who put forward a plea like that. Art is, indeed, in a sense, above and beyond the law: Acts of Parliament cannot control the artist's imagination; Courts of Law cannot compel him positively to write or paint this rather than that; and where the State prevents him from publishing anything that is not acceptable to those in power (as it can do, and as it actually does in totalitarian countries) we feel that there is something not only wrong but shameful about the spectacle of 'Art made tongue-tied by authority.'

All this is true; but artists, none the less, live in the same world as ordinary men, and if they want to publish their work or to put it into general circulation they can't be exempted, simply on the ground that they are artists, from the laws that regulate society. When I say they can't be exempted, 'can't,' in this context, is literally true; for

251

if the artist does claim exemption on that ground, he is confronted with an impossibility that is—as it were—built into his case. The law, he insists, must not be allowed to pronounce upon any alleged indecency in his work, because it is a work of art; the court must not be granted jurisdiction over him, because he is an artist. But what authority is to decide whether he and his work qualify for the claimed exemption? What but the law, operating by means of an Act of Parliament and administered by the courts? It is only by the law that anyone can be exempted from the law. The result of the artist's plea, therefore, if it were acceded to, would simply be to bring in the detested machinery at an earlier stage. And this would surely make matters worse, not better; for it must be even more intolerable for the artist that the law should decide the fundamental question whether he is an artist, than that it should decide the incidental question whether one of his works is outrageously indecent. But to say that the law may not pronounce upon his claim to the status of artist, and still to insist upon his right as an artist to exemption from censorial restrictions, is really to make the claim to be an artist a self-validating claim—if it is put forward it must be admitted—and to do this is tantamount to saying that in order to do justice to the claim of art there should, in the field of books and magazines and films and plays and pictures, be no restrictive legislation at all, or at any rate, none based on grounds of decency or morality.

Many of those who oppose censorship today would, of course, accept this conclusion—nor would they base their acceptance of it upon the view that the artist as such is entitled to any special privilege. Indeed, it is becoming rather old-fashioned nowadays to think of Art as a special kind of activity and to regard the artist as a special kind of person, entitled to extraordinary treatment. The line separating what is Art from what is not has worn as thin as the lines that used to separate one art from another: 'We are all artists now'; and Art comprises every kind of happening or object, from the impersonal products of aleatory machines to the crudest results of uninhibited self-expression. Portraits of the artist's mother [*Mère de l'Artiste*] have gone out of fashion—a point nicely made by the organizers of a recent exhibition in Paris, which included an object, under a glass dome, labelled (correctly) *Merde de l'Artiste*—evidently a literal proof of the thesis that to produce a work of art an artist need do no more than just express himself.

The case, then, against censorial legislation in the field of books and pictures and plays and films must really be based, not upon high-flown appeals to the sacredness of Art or to the liberty of the individual, not upon *a priori* principles, but upon more pragmatic grounds. Society, it is said, loses more than it gains by the imposition of such laws; if you tell people who want to write or to paint or to produce a film or a play that they must not publish or exhibit anything that outrages contemporary sensibilities, you will deprive them of the freedom they need if they are to fulfil themselves as artists and give the world their best work: you don't only prevent them from publishing the indecent works at which the prohibitory law is aimed (which may themselves be supreme works of art, and which in a generation or so may be no longer thought to be indecent), but you cramp them, as it were, all round; an artist simply cannot work in fetters.

Therefore (the argument continues) the law should refrain from intruding upon the field of art and literature, not because the artist can claim a specially privileged position, but simply in the interests of society, which is enriched by the things that the artist produces and correspondingly impoverished if he is not allowed to produce them. On this view, in order to assure to creative writers the freedom that they need, we ought to put up with the unrestricted publication of indecent, obscene, and pornographic matter: whatever benefit may result from suppressing it, society will on balance, it is claimed, be a loser.

To adjudicate upon this claim, one would have to weigh the loss to the world of literature and art that would result from the prohibition of grossly indecent works against the damage that would be inflicted on society if no restriction were placed upon them. Under a system of censorship, literature perhaps would suffer: some writers and painters might feel inhibited, some masterpieces might remain unwritten, or might have to wait for publication (like Joyce's *Ulysses*) until prevailing standards changed. Against that one must set the suffering that would be inflicted upon individual sensibilities, and the damage that would be done to society at large, by removing all control over the publication of indecency, obscenity, and pornography. That damage is of two kinds. Over and above the outrage inflicted upon the sensibilities of ordinary people, to protect which should—I suggest—be the primary aim of censorial legislation, there is the positive influence for bad that the publication of indecent books and films may have upon those who read or see them. Since the possibility of such influence is often denied by opponents of censorship, I must explain carefully what I mean by it. I should have thought that it went without saying that we may be influenced—particularly when we are young, but also after we have grown up—by things we read or see; sometimes we are conscious of this

255

influence, sometimes not; it operates, I should say, in varying degrees, sometimes for the better, sometimes for the worse. To be specific: it seems to me undeniable that, if we have read a book or poem or have seen a play or a film, our attitude to life may be altered by what we have read or seen—may be different from what it would have been if we had not read that book or poem, or seen that play or film. And what we read or see may affect not only our character but also our conduct: we may actually be impelled to go and do something that we saw enacted on the screen or read about in a book. The influence may be deep and lasting, or it may be trivial and temporary; it may be for the better, or it may be for the worse. A poem or a play may be either degrading or exalting in its effect; but that poems and plays do influence peoples' lives and conduct is, I should have thought, undeniable.

Of course, it is impossible to prove the truth of this proposition or to support it by precise statistics, either generally or in relation to a particular work. The same book or picture may leave some people unaffected, and may affect one person in one way, another in another; we can't say, therefore, that a particular film (for instance) will have a good or bad influence upon all the people who see it, or even upon an ascertainable proportion of them; nor can we say in advance that it will have a good or bad influence upon any particular person; nor, after a particular person has seen the film, can we gauge mathematically the extent of its influence upon him. And even if it does appear pretty plainly that a person was impelled to do something by (say) a film that he had seen—if, for instance (and this was a real case), a youth batters an old tramp to death or rapes a girl shortly after having seen a similar incident enacted in *A Clockwork Orange*—it is always possible to say that it was a coincidence: you can't prove that he wouldn't have battered the old tramp to death or raped the girl even if he hadn't seen the film. Even if he himself says, 'It was seeing the film that made me do it,' he may be self-deceived, or he may be seeking to transfer to others the responsibility for his act.

Now this general proposition, that things we read or see may influence us for better or worse, does not seem to me to be invalidated in the very least by our inability to offer a scientific proof of its truth, either generally or in relation to a particular work, or by our inability to support it by statistical evidence. To ask for scientific proof or statistical demonstration in such a case sounds, no doubt, impressive—it sounds as if the person asking for such proof was himself being scientific, when in fact his attitude and his approach are not scientific but the reverse: he is asking for a kind of proof, which, from the nature of the case, it is impossible to supply.

If one person is in love with another, his emotion will surely influence his attitude, his judgment, and his actions in relation to that person. It would be foolish (and, indeed, unscientific) to ask for a scientific definition of love or for a demonstration of the truth of the proposition that it influences people as I have suggested. And it would be wrong to say that the impossibility of providing such a demonstration and supporting it by statistical evidence shows that people are not really influenced in their relations with other people by their feelings from them.

Besides the direct influence of the unrestricted exhibition of indecent or obscene or sadistic art, we must consider also the indirect results. If one wants to get a fair idea of what those indirect results would be, one must take into account not only their impact upon those who actually read the books or see the film that contain them, but the effect that would be wrought upon people generally by the unrestricted publication and presentation of such things and the knowledge that their presentation and publication was permitted by law. In making one's estimate of that effect one has to rely on one's sense of how people's views are influenced, without their being aware of it, by what goes on around them, by the atmosphere of the society they live in.

I should say that the unrestricted circulation in the bookshops and on the bookstalls of grossly indecent and sadistic books and magazines, and the unrestricted presentation in theatres and cinemas of grossly indecent and sadistic films and live performances, coupled with the knowledge that these things were permitted by the law of the land, would make a difference to the way the general public regard the indecent and the inhumane, particularly in the field of sex and violence. People would unconsciously re-define these concepts, and alter their attitude towards the things they stand for: accepted standards of decency and humanity would themselves be modified; things that today disgust us by their indecency would no longer seem indecent, things that today horrify us by their brutality would no longer seem brutal, or not so shockingly brutal as they do now. The quality of life would in these respects undergo a gradual metamorphosis.

I say 'a gradual metamorphosis,' but I don't think that the process would be likely to be a slow one: people's attitudes and opinions on social questions nowadays change ever more swiftly, and nowhere more swiftly, it seems, than in this very field. If one wants to appreciate how rapid and how radical the change can be, one has only to switch on the television, or turn the pages of a newspaper, or visit a theatre or a cinema. Things are described, language is used, scenes are depicted or enacted, that couldn't conceivably have found a place in print or on the screen or on the stage, twenty, ten, or even half-a-dozen years ago. There are for instance, films that shock the ordinarily sensitive person (though they may delight others) by their representation of cruelty or violence—films like *A Clockwork Orange*, or *Straw Dogs*, or *The Devils*, or *Beyond the Valley of the Dolls* (which was, in effect, a re-enactment of the killing of Sharon Tate and her friends by the fiend Charles Manson's pack of murderesses). Other films contain scenes of castration or coprophilia, or vivid presentations of sexual intercourse, normal or perverse; in Bertolucci's *Last Tango in Paris*, for instance, Marlon Brando, in full view of the audience, reached for the butter and used it as a lubricant, to facilitate an act that a few years ago, in the law-suit concerning *Lady Chatterley's Lover*, was deemed unmentionable.

I am not at the moment concerned with the question whether the change is for the better or the worse: I merely draw attention to the pace at which it is taking place. Here I should perhaps repeat that, though I believe that seeing obscenities in books or films may affect people's character and conduct, and will certainly affect people's attitude towards obscenity generally, this is not my primary reason for saying that their publication should be subject to control by law. What I propose is that the publication of obscenities should be prohibited in cases where it would transgress accepted standards of decency and humanity, and so outrage people's sensibilities; it is the outrage upon people's sensibilities, not the effect it would have upon their characters or their behaviour, that affords, in my opinion, the primary reason for holding that their publication should be restrained by the law.

I have posed the question whether the law should intervene in the field of indecency and obscenity, in art, in literature, in conduct; I have reviewed, very summarily, the arguments on either side; and I have outlined my reasons for holding that the law should so intervene.

I should like to conclude by touching upon a question that goes a little deeper—a question not so much for the lawyer as for the social anthropologist or the psychologist. The claim that the law should not intervene in the field of indecency is put forward, not of course by or on behalf of the decadent, the dissolute, the prurient, or the pornographers—though they may be its incidental and illegitimate beneficiaries. No: it is put forward by intellectuals and the *avant-garde*, to vindicate the right of the individual to express himself, to do his own thing, without interference or inhi-bition. What is the impulse, the motive force, behind this individualistic pressure? It is a claim for a kind of liberty—the liberty to say what you like—for free speech. But it is in no sense political, though it is seized on and turned to their own purposes by social revolutionaries, like Professor Marcuse, who recommends the methodical use of obscenities as a revolutionary tool or weapon: to shock the Establishment is one way of shaking the Establishment. No: the pressure for liberty of self-expression is surely—like the egalitarian and humanitarian tendencies that were the subjects of my first two lectures—the expression of a mood of disenchantment with the social and economic order, of a desire to assert the claim of the in-dividual in a world of combines and corporations, to vindicate the virtues of nature in the world of conventions and constraints, to do justice to those who wish, in a world of universal competition, not to surpass others, but simply to be them-selves. What I have tried to do in these three lectures is to focus attention upon one or two points at which civilization itself seems to be threatened by contemporary tendencies—ten-dencies not in themselves deleterious, tendencies which if restrained within certain limits are actu-ally civilizing tendencies, but which are dangerous if they are carried too far.

First, civilization depends upon the recognition and the cultivation of excellences and superiorities; the maintenance of a civilized society, therefore, would be made impossible by a thorough-going egalitarianism. Competition in excellence is a civilizing force, and you do not discredit it by calling it a rat-race.

Second, civilization depends upon the maintenance of law and order, and law and order can't be maintained, in an imperfect world, without resort of force. Humanity, in the sense of humaneness, is not self-sustaining. You do not discredit force by calling it brute force.

Finally, civilized society exists for the individual—we can't remind ourselves of that too often in an age when the state has grown top-heavy, and seems to crush all individual effort, all individual character, to leave us little room to fulfil ourselves: no wonder there exists today an almost desperate craving for self-expression. But society is pluralistic, and each individual must respect the individuality of his fellow-citizens; he must exercise self-restraint, out of respect not only for the rights but for the feelings of his fellow-men; self-expression is not self-validating, and affords no sovereign plea in its own defence when it collides with the common feelings and susceptibilities of society.